Revised third edition

Don Pedro
presents...

POLITICS & PROTEST

Bristol: subvertising | graffiti | stickers | posters

This book is dedicated to Will Brown, 1959-2010.
A genuine-to-the-core political activist and artist,
and much missed.

INTRODUCTION 4
GOVERNMENT 6
OCCUPY 18
HUMAN RIGHTS 20
EU REFERENDUM 26
UKIP 29
GENERAL ELECTION 2017 30
NHS 36
CAPITALISM 38
ENVIRONMENT 48
LEFT AND RIGHT 58
RICH AND POOR 64
RACISM 68
SHOP/CONSUME 70
HOUSING 78
WAR 80
REFUGEES AND MIGRANTS 88
BILLBOARDS AND ADVERTISING 92
WOMEN 100
ANIMALS 104
CLASS WAR 108
BUSH AND BLAIR 112
ARMS TRADE 118
PALESTINE 122
TRUMP 124
CARS 126
ELECTIONS 2005 AND 2010 134
AUSTERITY AND CUTS 136
POLICE 140
BRISTOL ISSUES 142
AND THE REST 146

INTRODUCTION TO THE 3RD EDITION

I'm a serial photographer – over time images accumulate into series, and this is one of them: politics and protest.

These street photographs span 1999 to 2017 - featuring subvertising*, graffiti, posters and stickers, speaking directly to anyone who's looking.

Most of the images were taken in Bristol, as I move around on foot or by bike. I document images whether they match my own view of the world or not, and irrespective of offensiveness.

The categories I've used in this book just provide a loose structure. Many images could easily fit into several categories.

This edition adds 32 extra pages and over 180 new photos. The cover is now gold, for its association with wealth and power.

Don Pedro
When my daughters were little they asked what Pete was in Spanish. They added the 'Don' without realising it's a courteous form of address. They've since dropped the Don, but I haven't.

Flickr
At www.flickr.com/photos/donpedro you can see these images and the hundreds that didn't make it into the book via the 'Albums' link.

*Subvertising: subverting an existing advert by adding letters or images to change its meaning. Or creating an advert which looks familiar, but which has an unexpectedly different message.

My thanks to the St Just Mob, whose subvertising features strongly throughout the book.

The recent political landscape

At the time of the book's inception (summer 2009) MPs had been uncovered misbehaving with their expenses (Tony Blair's expenses were shredded 'by mistake'). Labour were entering their 13th and final year in power, and the banks had been bailed out after helping create a global financial crisis.

When the second edition was published (November 2011) the Conservative and Liberal coalition government was under way, delivering its promise of large-scale cuts in public spending.

At the time of writing (August 2017) the Brexit negotiations have started, uncertainty and complications abound. We have another Conservative coalition government, following the 2017 General Election.

New types of leaders are being chosen as distrust grows for the political establishment. Donald Trump in the US. Macron in France. Jeremy Corbyn here.

Migration is a divisive issue here and across much of Europe.
Islamic extremists ISIL/ISIS are at war in Syria and Iraq.
Terrorist attacks around the world are increasingly common.

Social media and the internet have an increasing and complex role in political change.

Meanwhile the environmental clock keeps ticking.
Time to get political?

Don Pedro (aka Pete Maginnis)
August 2017

GOVERNMENT...

I like this quote from Tony Benn on the nature of political struggle. The sentiment is echoed in images throughout this book.

"Every generation had to fight the same battles as their ancestors had to fight, again and again, for there is no final victory and no final defeat. Two flames have burned from the beginning of time - the flame of anger against injustice and the flame of hope..."

Tony Benn, Letters to my Grandchildren

[Tony Benn was an MP in Bristol South East and Bristol East for 30 years]

NO LEADERS
FOR THE
FREE

Performance and economy:
a perfect coalition.
UNLIKE THE CON-DEMS
VAUXHALL
primesight

new
NESCAFÉ
IT'S A STATE OF
CONTROL
Mills
Allen

WHAT THIS
COUNTRY NEEDS IS
MORE UNEMPLOYED
POLITICIANS.

BRISTOL RESISTANCE
DON'T VOTE,
ORGANISE!
http://bristolresistance.blogspot.com

Tollgate
VOTE NOBODY
More O'Ferrall

Corruptisima republica
plurimae leges.
Tacitus

VOTE OR RIOT?
YOU DECIDE

Socialist Worker
Cameron—resign now
HE'S
GOT
TO GO
Kick the Tories out

Top row from left - 2005: No leaders for the free | 2010: A perfect coalition – unlike the Con-Dems | 2000: It's a state of control | Middle row – 2014: What this country needs is more unemployed politicians [www.wapiti.se, www.activedistribution.org] | 2010: Don't vote, organise! | 2001: Vote nobody | Bottom row – 2009: Corruptisima republica plurimae leges [the quote from Roman historian Tacitus translates as 'The more corrupt the state the more numerous the laws] | 2010: Vote or riot? You decide | 2016: He's got to go [PM David Cameron in April 2016] |

THE LABOUR PARTY HAS
ADOPTED THE CONDOM AS IT'S
OFFICIAL EMBLEM
IT STANDS FOR INFLATION.
STOPS PRODUCTION.
GIVES COVER TO A BUNCH
OF PRICKS.
AND GIVES ONE A FALSE
SENSE OF SECURITY WHILST
BEING STUFFED.
IN 1997 TONY BLAIR PROMISED US
MORE POLICE, TEACHERS, NURSES,
DOCTORS, TO CUT WAITING LISTS, TO
CUT RED TAPE.
WHAT DID WE GET NONE OF THE
ABOVE, BUT WE DID GET HIGHER
INDIRECT TAXES, TONY'S CRONIES.
ASK YOURSELF WHY GO TO THE
COUNTRY 4 YEARS INTO A 5 YEAR
PARLIAMENT. IS THERE A WINTER
OF DISCONTENT COMING AS WITH
THE LAST LABOUR GOVERNMENT!!
ONLY YOUR VOTE AND TIME WILL TELL.

2004: The Labour Party has adopted the condom as it's official emblem.

It stands for inflation. Stops production. Gives cover to a bunch of pricks.

And gives one a false sense of security whilst being stuffed.

In 1997 Tony Blair promised us more police, teachers, nurses, doctors, to cut waiting lists, to cut red tape.

What did we get none of the above, but we did get higher indirect taxes, Tony's cronies. Ask yourself why go to the country 4 years into a 5 year Parliament. Is there a winter of discontent coming as with the last Labour government!! Only your vote and time will tell.

[The Winter of Discontent was in 1978–1979, when local authority trade unions went on strike for better pay whilst the Labour government of James Callaghan sought to hold a pay freeze to control inflation]

VOTE
4
ANIMALS
election
2010
www.vote4animals.org.uk

2010: Vote 4 animals [www.vote4animals.org.uk]

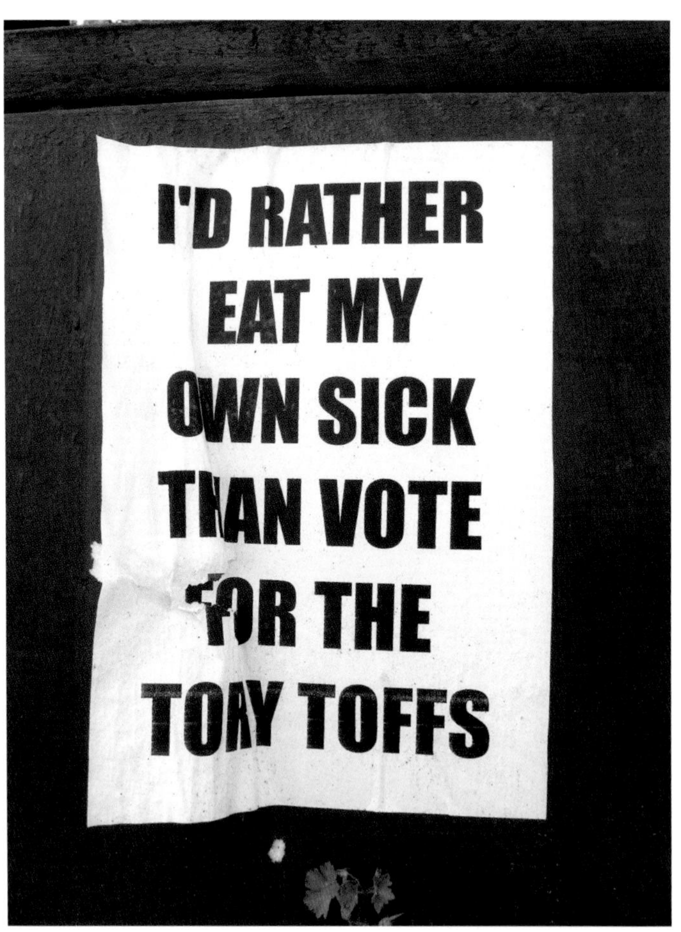
I'D RATHER
EAT MY
OWN SICK
THAN VOTE
FOR THE
TORY TOFFS

2010: I'd rather eat sick than vote for the Tory toffs

NOTA FACTS
"A VOTE FOR THE LADS"

2010: A vote for the lads [Nota Facts produced some unusual and memorable 2010 election commentaries]

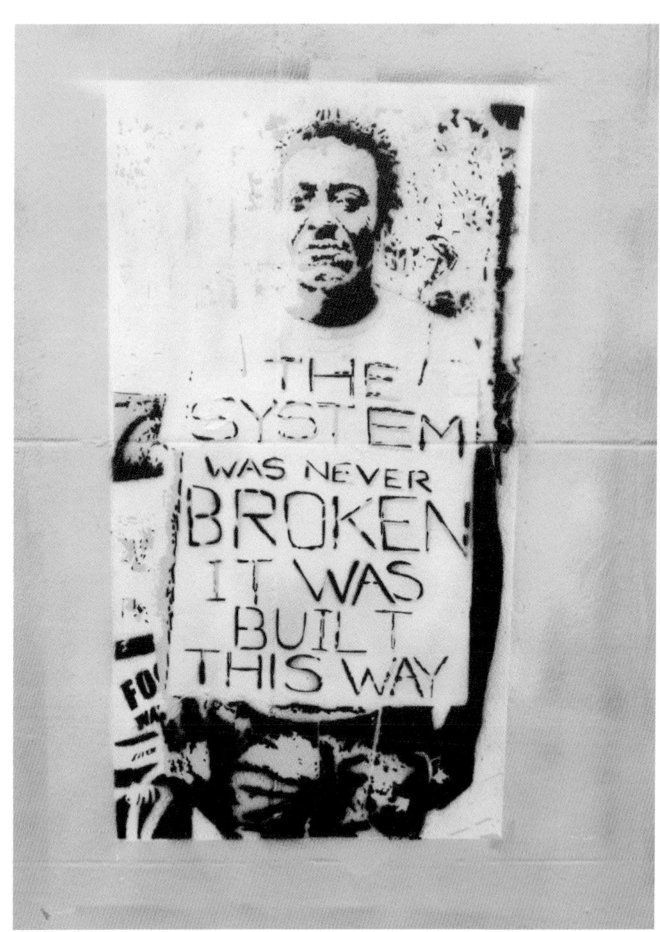
THE SYSTEM
WAS NEVER
BROKEN
IT WAS
BUILT
THIS WAY

2017: The system was never broken it was built this way

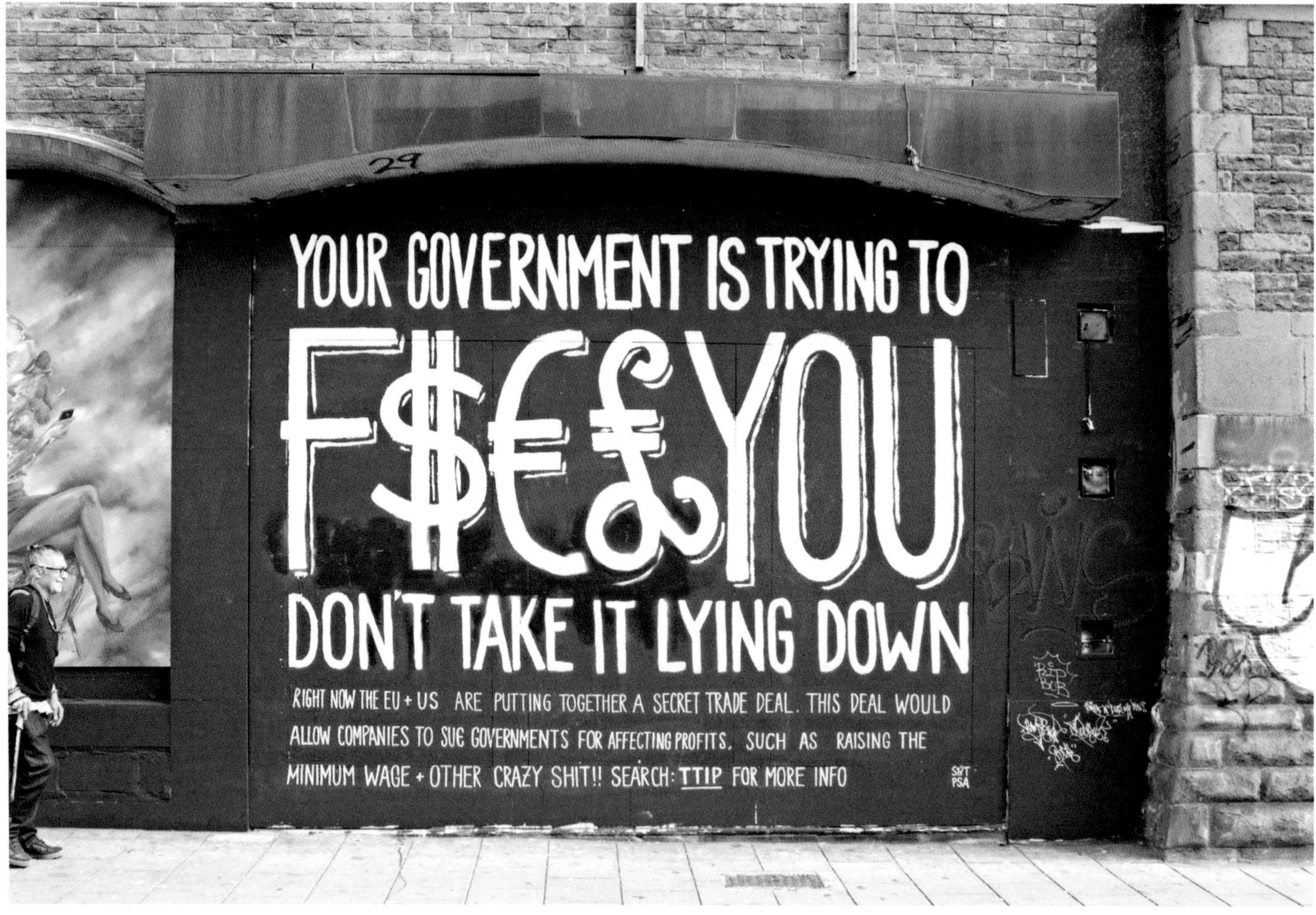
29
YOUR GOVERNMENT IS TRYING TO
F$€£YOU
DON'T TAKE IT LYING DOWN
RIGHT NOW THE EU + US ARE PUTTING TOGETHER A SECRET TRADE DEAL. THIS DEAL WOULD
ALLOW COMPANIES TO SUE GOVERNMENTS FOR AFFECTING PROFITS. SUCH AS RAISING THE
MINIMUM WAGE + OTHER CRAZY SHIT!! SEARCH: TTIP FOR MORE INFO
S&T
PSA

2014: Your government is trying to F$€£ you [This proposed secretive EU-US trade deal has far-reaching adverse consequences for the environment, employment rights, safety laws, the NHS]

"DEMOCRACY"

THESE PEOPLE COULD CHANGE
EVERYTHING
15.7M
DID NOT VOTE
11.3M
TORIES
9.3M
LABOUR
3.9M
UKIP
3.8M
OTHER
2.4M
LIB DEM
VOTE
"IT AIN'T MUCH, BUT ITS ALL WE HAVE AGAINST THE GREEDHEADS"
Hunter S. Thompson

PASSIVE RESISTANCE 1
BRITISH EMPIRE 0
"I BELIEVE GANDHI IS THE ONLY PERSON WHO KNEW ABOUT REAL DEMOCRACY – NOT DEMOCRACY AS THE RIGHT TO GO AND BUY WHAT YOU WANT, BUT DEMOCRACY AS THE RESPONSIBILITY TO BE ACCOUNTABLE TO EVERYONE AROUND YOU."
VANDANA SHIVA
NON VIOLENT REVOLUTION

DEMOCRACY
"IS THE WORST FORM OF GOVERNMENT IN THE WORLD, EXCEPT ALL THOSE OTHER FORMS THAT HAVE BEEN TRIED FROM TIME TO TIME"
WINSTON CHURCHILL

Clockwise from top left – 2016: "Democracy" | 2017: Hunter S. Thompson on voting | 2017: Winston Churchill on democracy | 2013: Vandana Shiva on democracy |

GOD IS
GOOD.
BRISTOLCITY
COUNCIL
THE BIG CONSPIRACY
THE GREATEST
COVER-UP

THE BRISTOL PAMPHLETEERS No 1
TONY BLAIR (PRIME MINISTER).
"EDUCATION, EDUCATION, EDUCATION".
REFERENCE LIBRARIES AND MUSEUMS ARE A VITAL AND INTEGRAL PART OF EDUCATION AND SHOULD BE FUNDED AS SUCH.
BRISTOL CITY COUNCIL: cuts, cuts cuts !!!
CUTTING THE SERVICES YOU WANT, CUTTING THE SERVICES YOU NEED!
BRISTOLIANS SAY: SAVE OUR SERVICES, AND OUR FACILITIES!
Write to Tony Blair* to tell him how you dislike the undemocratic, secretive and morally corrupt way that the city council run Bristol.
* The Rt Hon Tony Blair MP (Prime Minister) C/O 10 Downing Street London, SW1A 2AA. Fax:0171 270 0196.
...HAVE YOUR SAY; VOTE IN MAY TO CHANGE THE CITY COUNCIL.
PUBLISHED IN THE SPIRIT OF EDMUND BURKE 1774 1780 "THE GREATEST GOOD FOR THE GREATEST NUMBER"

THE BRISTOL PHAMPHLETEERS No5
BRISTOL CITY COUNCIL:
INCOMPETENT , INEFFECIENT, INEFFECTIVE
TO REMOVE THE CURRENT CITY COUNCIL
HAVE YOUR SAY VOTE IN MAY !
If you dislike the way the City Council is run Fax Tony Blair @ 10 Downing Street
FAX 0171 270 0196
Published by the angry voters of Bristol

1999: The council under attack

Left - 2003: I'm told that a man in dispute with the council over the loss of his council house lived in this structure for several years.

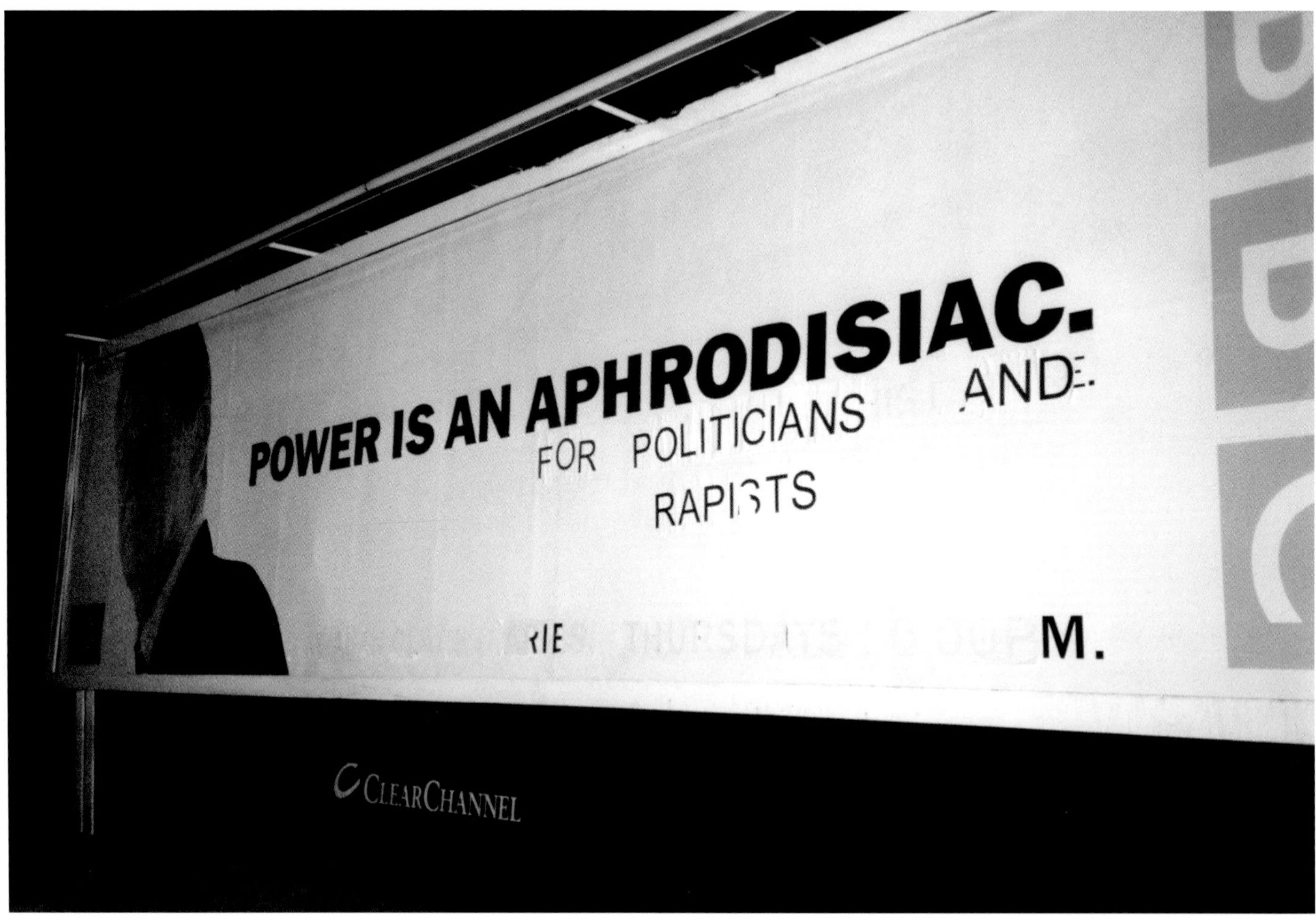
POWER IS AN APHRODISIAC.
FOR POLITICIANS AND
RAPISTS
M.
CLEARCHANNEL

2004: Power is an aphrodisiac for politicians and rapists

YOUTH! STUDY THE 3 PRINCIPLES OF MINISTER GOVE
SELF-DISCIPLINE. ENTREPRENEURSHIP. COMPETITION!

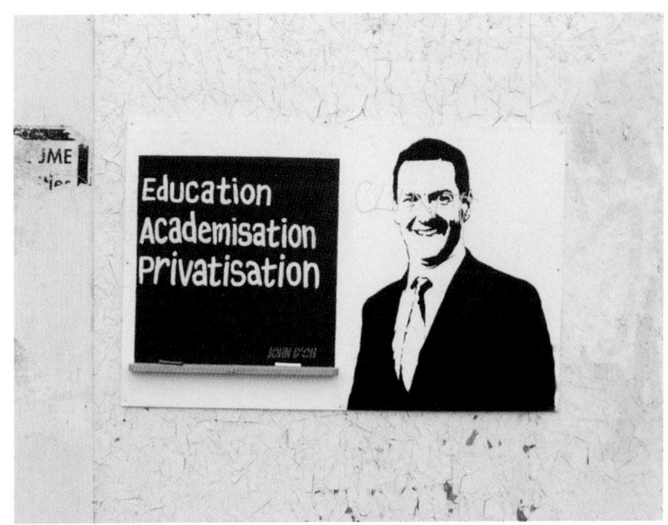
Education
Academisation
Privatisation

CONSERVATIVE
HYPOCRITICAL
AVARICIOUS
VULGAR
The real thugs terrorising Britain

TORY
DUP
Just SAY NO
RESPECT
WOMEN
LGBTQA+

Clockwise from top left - 2013: Youth! Study the 3 principles of Minister Gove | 2016: Education, Academisation, Privatisation [Chancellor George Osborne] | 2017: Just say no [to the Conservative coalition with the Democratic Unionist Party, whose respect for women, the environment, LGBTQA and diversity is questioned] | 2016: CHAV [George Osborne, David Cameron, Iain Duncan Smith]|

OCCUPY...

The Occupy movement is an international socio-political movement against social and economic inequality and lack of "real democracy" around the world, its primary goal being to advance social and economic justice and new forms of democracy. Source: Wikipedia

WHO ARE: BILDERBERG? CFR? TRILATERAL
COMMISSION?
TAVISTOCK INSTITUTE? MERCHANT VENTURERS?
COMMON PURPOSE? CARLYLE GROUP? CLUB OF
ROCKERFELLER FOUNDATION? ROME?
RHODES SOCIETY? PNAC? REDSHIELD?
BOHEMIA GROVE? JEKYLE ISLAND?
NEW WORLD ORDER?

2012: Who are: Bilderberg? CFR? Trilateral Commisssion?

SAT October 15th 2011.
Occupation in protest of
"the system".
Peacefully Occupy the LONDON
Stock Exchange at 4:30pm until
December 12th 2011 at 11am. at :-
10, paternoster Square, LONDON.
For more info :- Google ~ Global Revolution
day Oct 15th 2011. or check-out
events on Face-book.

Occupy
Nottingham
The 1%. that are destroy-
ing the Planet, Stealing our
money, our jobs, our homes, our
education, THEY are the RICH,
the BANKERS, the POLITICIANS.
CAMERON
OUR CITY
IS IN OUR
HANDS

DEBENHAMS
DEBENHAMS
CAMERON
OUR CITY
IS IN YOUR
HANDS
THE ELITE RULING CLASS WANT US
ASLEEP SO WE'LL STAY DOCILE, AN APATHETIC
HERD OF PASSIVE CONSUMERS NONE PARTICIPANTS
IN THE TRUE AGENDA OF OUR GOVERNMENTS -
WHICH IS TO KEEP US SEPERATE AND PRESENT
AN IMAGE OF A WORLD FILLED WITH
PROBLEMS, THAT THEY AND ONLY THEY MAY
ONE DAY, SOMEWHERE IN THE NEVER-ARRIVING
FUTURE BE ABLE TO SOLVE...
JUST STAY ASLEEP, KEEP WATCHING TV.
BILL HICKS

WE
ARE
THE
99%

Clockwise from top left - 2011: Occupy the London Stock Exchange | 2011: Occupy Nottingham | 2011: We are the 99% | 2012: The elite ruling class… [Quote from Bill Hicks, American comedian and social critic] |

HUMAN RIGHTS...

CHINA
China is thought to have the highest number of political prisoners of any country in the world. Human rights activists counted 742 arrests in 2007 alone.
BRAVE AND FORGOTTEN WHILE WE KEEP BUYING CHEAP GOODS
There is no way of knowing the total number of people behind bars for "endangering state security". Punishment for this charge ranges from torture to capital punishment.

2013: China

BIGGER. FATTER. GYPSIER.
DALE FARMIER
14.02.12
Sponsored by
HONDA
The Power of Dreams
JCDecaux

2012: Dale Farmier [The traveller site at Dale Farm featured in the Channel 4 series 'Big Fat Gypsy Weddings'. Travellers there lost a 10 year legal battle and were evicted in October 2011]

Open your eyes to 3
EQUALITY For DAD'S!
Video mobile is here

2003: Justice for dads

Left – 2003: Equality for dads

[Fathers 4 Justice were active at this time. In one 2003 incident two campaigners scaled the Royal Courts of Justice, dressed as Batman and Robin. The stencil shows Michael Douglas in the film 'Falling Down', about to go on a violent rampage having been pushed to his limits]

PRIVACY IS A
HUMAN RIGHT

IN PRISON MY
WHOLE LIFE

NON-VIOLENT
REVOLUTION
FREE MUMIA

FREE THE
COLNBROOK HUNGER
STRIKERS
DEAN ST. BS2

Clockwise from top left - 2006: Privacy is a human right | 2012: In prison my whole life [Refers to the 2008 film of the same name. Mumia Abu-Jamal was on death row in Pennsylvania for almost 30 years. His death sentence was commuted in 2011 to life imprisonment without parole] | 2006: Free the Colnbrook hunger strikers [Up to 150 detainees at Colnbrook, a detention centre for asylum seekers, went on hunger strike in protest against their likely deportation] | 2002: Free Mumia [Mumia Abu-Jamal, see above] |

Human rights...

2010: This is a protest - human rights! [This gentleman told me that he had been under 24 hour surveillance for the last 4 years by the government, who had forced him to close his chip shop. He maintains a daily protest]

EU REFERENDUM...

NOT #INFOR THIS?
REGISTER TO VOTE ON THE EU REFERENDUM NOW!
WWW.
WEAREEUROPE.
ORG.UK

2016: Not #inforthis? [Donald Trump and then Foreign Secretary Boris Johnson. www.weareeurope.org.uk]

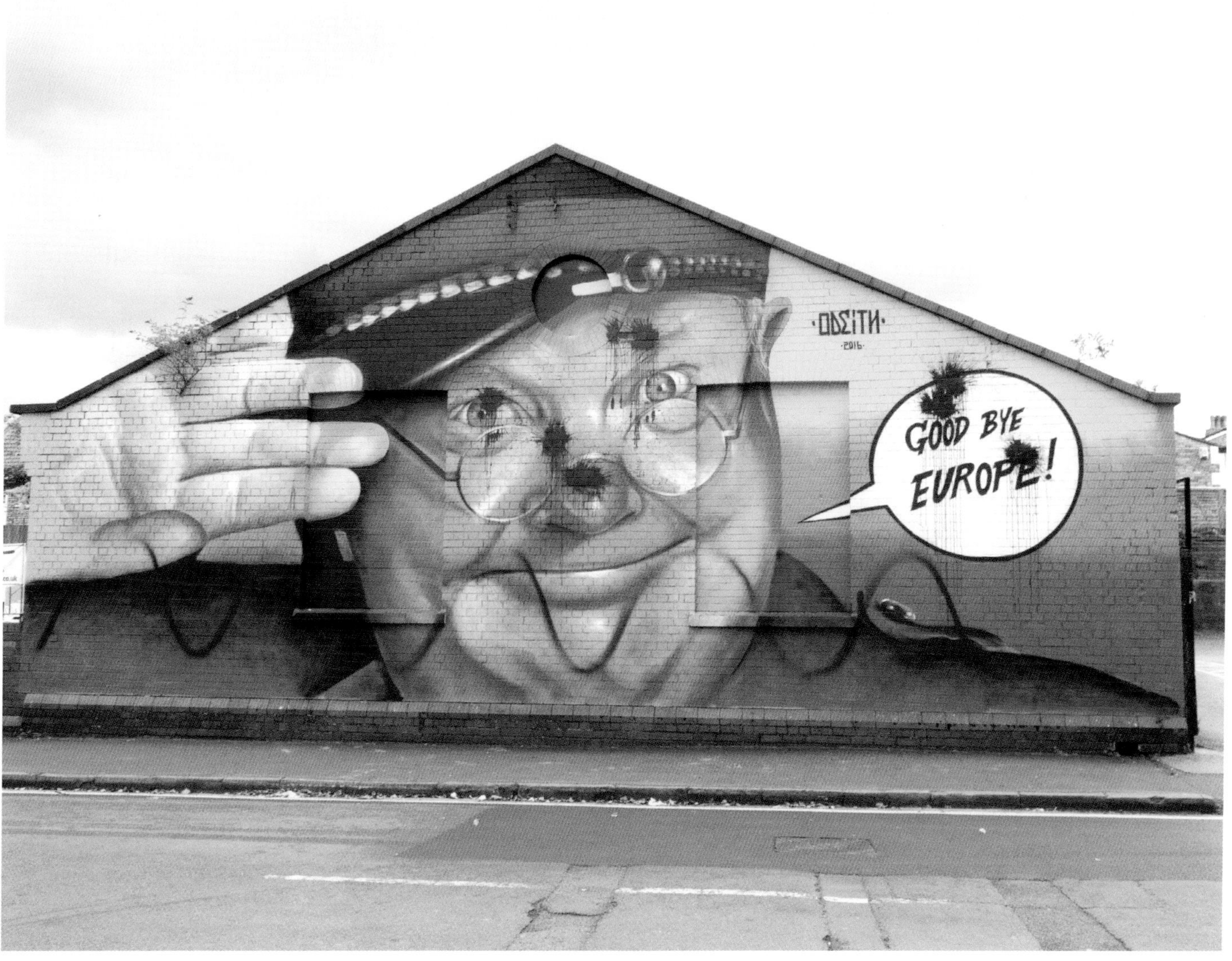
GOOD BYE
EUROPE!

2016: Good bye Europe!

LOVE EUROPE
LEAVE THE EU
BRITAIN OUT
GET BRITAIN OUT OF THE EU
ON JUNE 23rd
VOTE LEAVE

EU CITIZENS
WELCOME
#RightToStay

VOTE X
REMAIN
23 JUNE
Labour
labourinforbritain.org.uk

EUR PE
VOTE STAY
LOOKING
ATTRACTIVE NOW?

I wasn't asked and I don't want it ..
I REJECT EU CITIZENSHIP
If you don't want it either, tel 0800 587 6 587
UKIP
www.ukip.org

STAY IN EUROPE TO
CHANGE EUROPE
VOTE 'IN' ON 23 JUNE
STAY IN EUROPE TO
CHANGE EUROPE
VOTE 'IN' ON 23 JUNE

Let's give our NHS the
£350 million
the EU takes every week
Vote Leave, take control on 23 June

#Lexit
The Left Leave Campaign
No to a bosses' Europe
No to fortress Europe
No to TTIP

VOTE
LOVE
#REASONSTOREMAIN
#VOTEREMAIN

All from 2016. Top row from left - Britain out of the EU [www.britainfirst.org]| EU citizens welcome | Vote remain 23 June [labourinforbritain.org.uk] | Middle row - Europe, looking attractive now? | I reject EU citizenship | Stay in Europe to change Europe [www.anothereurope.org] | Bottom row - Let's give our NHS the £350 million the EU takes every week | #Lexit The Left Leave Campaign [www.leftleave.org] | Vote love |

UKIP...

From the time of the 2014 and 2015 local elections, at the height of UKIP's popularity. The pressure they placed on the Conservative government contributed to the decision to hold the EU referendum.

SOFT DRINKS SOLD HERE
Nigel Farage will give Britain its voice back.
TAKE BACK CONTROL OF OUR COUNTRY. VOTE UKIP 22nd MAY.
JCDecaux

Oy! Nigel Farage!
UPRICK
UKIP PARTY MEMBERS ARE OFTEN VILE, SEXIST, RACIST, HOMOPHOBIC, ETC., ETC.

PUBLIC HEALTH WARNING
PLEASE MIND THE FARAGE
BRISTOL C. C.
53.A

I'M NOT VOTING
ON MAY 22nd
UKIP
MORE LEAFLETS, THANK YOU
UKIP
Call 0800 587 6 587 or visit

2014: Nigel Farage will give Britain its voice back | 2014: Oy! Nigel Farage! | 2015: Please mind the farage [The winning entry in comedian Mark Thomas' competition to invent a definition of farage was 'the liquid found at the bottom of the bin or waste container'] | 2014: I'm not voting UKIP |

GENERAL ELECTION 2017...

2017: Voted them out of Bristol [The original 'vote them out' message was updated after the election, where Labour won all four seats in Bristol, taking Bristol North West from the Conservatives]

I AM A THREAT
TO YOUR LOCAL HOSPITAL
TO YOUR CHILD'S EDUCATION
TO YOUR STANDARD OF LIVING
TO YOUR JOB SECURITY
TO YOUR PENSION
TO YOUR PEACE & SECURITY
DON'T VOTE CONSERVATIVE ON JUNE 8TH
#TORIESOUT
THE PEOPLE'S ASSEMBLY
maxx
SMARTSCREEN

2017: I am a threat [This People's Assembly billboard appeared in 40 locations around the country]

18-35? IF YOU DONT VOTE, ANCIENT RELICS OF THE PAST WILL DECIDE YOUR FUTURE
#ENDMAYTHISJUNE

2017: 18 to 35?

2017: Jeremy Corbyn with halo

General election 2017…

TORIES
OUT!

#UseYourVote
#EnoughisEnough
#WhoFundsISIS
#Hypocrisy

STRONG AND STABLE DEALERSHIP
CONSERVATIVES
SHIT

CORBYN
FUTURE
VOTE FOR JUSTICE
LABOUR
8TH JUNE
FOR THE MANY NOT THE FEW

Clockwise from top left - 2017: Tories out! | 2017: #EnoughIsEnough #UseYourVote #WhoFundsISIS #Hypocrisy [emails from the US Obama administration named Saudi Arabia and Qatar as funders of Isis amongst others. Britain trades arms to Saudi Arabia] | 2017: Corbyn future | 2017: Strong and stable dealership |

Vote
Labour
Vote Labour labour.org.uk
KEEP
SANE
AND
DON'T
VOTE
TORY

ARBEIT MACHT FREI
Strong & Stable
LEARN TO
DO RIGHT
SEE THAT
JUSTICE
IS DONE
HELP THOSE
WHO ARE
OPPRESSED
Conservative
Labour

Let's make
June the
end of May

FOR THE
MANY
NOT THE
FOR THE
MANY
NOT THE
FEW
FOR THE

Clockwise from top left - 2017: Keep sane and don't vote Tory | 2017: Arbeit macht frei [a German phrase meaning "work sets you free". The slogan appears on the entrance of Nazi concentration camps. The Corbyn stencil is from a photo of his arrest protesting against South African apartheid in 1984] | 2017: For the many not the few [Jeremy Corbyn's election mantra] | 2017: Let's make June the end of May |

General election 2017…

STRONG
AND
STABLE
MY ARSE

2017: Strong and stable my arse [Theresa May's election mantra was 'strong and stable']

LAST CHANCE
SALOON!
THE BEST OFFER
ON THE TABLE
WE'VE HAD IN
OUR LIFETIME!
VOTE
LABOUR

2017: Last chance saloon [Location: outside my polling station]

NHS...

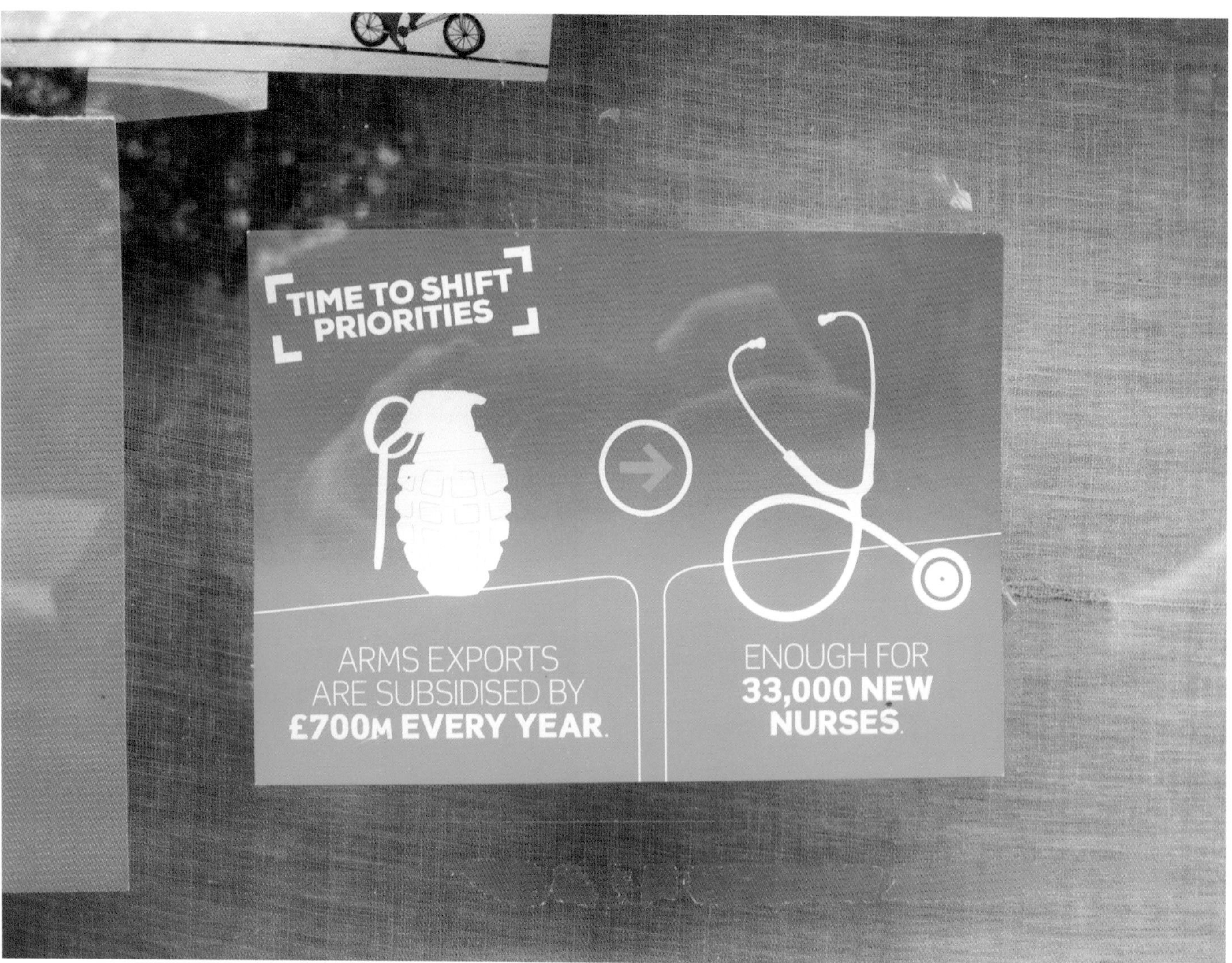
TIME TO SHIFT PRIORITIES
ARMS EXPORTS ARE SUBSIDISED BY £700M EVERY YEAR.
ENOUGH FOR 33,000 NEW NURSES.

2014: Time to shift priorities

NHS
FOR PEOPLE NOT FOR PROFIT

THE DOCTOR CAN'T SEE YOU NOW.
WAITING ROOM
THE TORIES HAVE MADE IT HARDER TO SEE A GP
YOUR VOTE CAN CHANGE THIS
Labour
I WOULDN'T

BIG AL SAYS:
NO JUNIOR DOCTOR CUTS

LAUGHTER MAY BE THE BEST MEDICINE BUT IT'S TIME TO SACK THE CLOWN
#SACKTHEHUNT

CHOOSE THE TORIES OR THE
NHS
YOU CAN'T HAVE BOTH!

KISSING THE NHS GOODBYE?

I support junior doctors
BMA

Dear Mr Cameron,
You're making a big mistake with the NHS.
Please, please listen to us.
66% of NHS staff think that if government plans go ahead they will make the NHS worse.

KEEP CALM AND SHOP INDEPENDENT IN

VOTE CONSERVATIVE
TO DESTROY OUR
NHS
VOTE LABOUR!
TO SAVE IT

Top row from left - 2017: For people not for profit | 2017: The doctor can't see you now | 2016: Big Al says no junior doctor cuts | Middle row - 2017: #sackthehunt [Jeremy Hunt, Secretary of State for Health] | 2017: Choose the Tories or the NHS | 2017: Kissing the NHS goodbye? [Donald Trump with Theresa May, concerns that trade treaties could allow US companies to buy into the health service] | Bottom row - 2016: I support junior doctors | 2012: Dear Mr Cameron [38degrees campaign against planned changes. 38degrees.org.uk/nhs] | 2017: Vote Conservative to destroy our NHS |

CAPITALISM...

Capitalism in its present form requires continuous generation of profit and economic growth, resulting in conflicts with our long-term needs. How can the environment cope with the effects of present levels of consumption? How can a value system which is motivated by profit produce outcomes that are good for the planet?

Yet trade deals like TTIP between the EU and the US are currently being negotiated. The basic premis is that liberalising trade will generate economic prosperity. Corporations will be allowed to sue governments over loss of profit, and the courts will operate in secret.

There are far reaching consequences for the environment, food safety, employment rights, the NHS, and for democracy itself.

If you don't know much about this disturbing shift of power towards corporations – look up TTIP.

DON'T LET BIG BUSINESS SUE THE UK
SAY NO TO TTIP
BENHAMS
Post

2016: Don’t let big business sue the UK. Say no to TTIP

BANKS
the
Still hating

NEW IRISH
PROVERB -
may you pay
less tax than
apple inc and
your glass be
always full.
#JOHN DOH

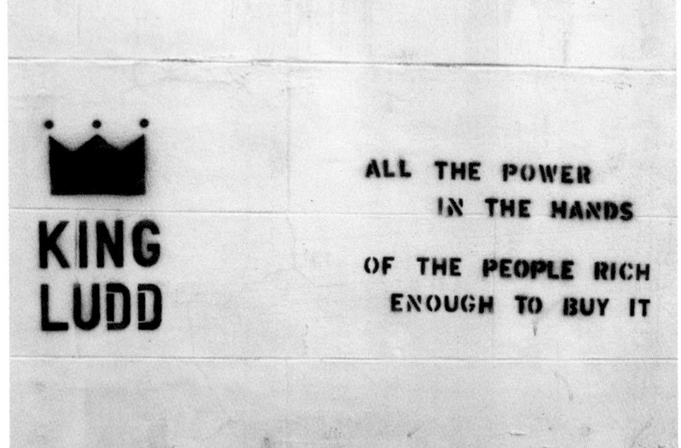
KING
LUDD
ALL THE POWER
IN THE HANDS
OF THE PEOPLE RICH
ENOUGH TO BUY IT

TTIP FREE ZONE
TTIP threatens local democracy, public services
and the environment. www.ttipfreezone.org.uk

Glam
Rocks!
M&S
money SUCKS
JCDecaux
BRISTOL CITY COUNCIL

STARBUCKS? VODAFHONE? AMAZON?
We're closing in on undeclared income
JCDecaux

action
don't just talk about capitalism !
fight it !
MAYDAY 2000
www.freespeech.org / mayday 2K
QUEER AS FOLK 2
Back with a bang
score
outdoor

Above - 2000: Don’t just talk about capitalism! Fight it!

Left – clockwise from top left - 2011: Still hating the banks | 2016: New Irish proverb [Apple moves revenue through its Irish Republic office where it pays lower corporation tax] | 2016: TTIP free zone [www.ttipfreezone.org.uk] | 2012: Starbucks? Vodafhone? Amazon? We’re closing in on undeclared income [Parliament’s Public Accounts Committee strongly denounced the tax avoidance of these and other giant companies, like Google] | 2010: Glam rocks! Money sucks | 2011: All the power in the hands of the people rich enough to buy it |

Next page – 2009: Find out why millions of people across Britain are unemployed

Find out why millions
across Britain ARE UNEMPLOY
Call into your local branch AND ASK US WHY ?
NatWest
JCDe

0141 01
of people
h us
m/millions
NatWest
GREEDY Banking
East Street Shopping
City Centre
Tobacco Factory
Greville Smyth Park
North Street
Geddes
Geddes

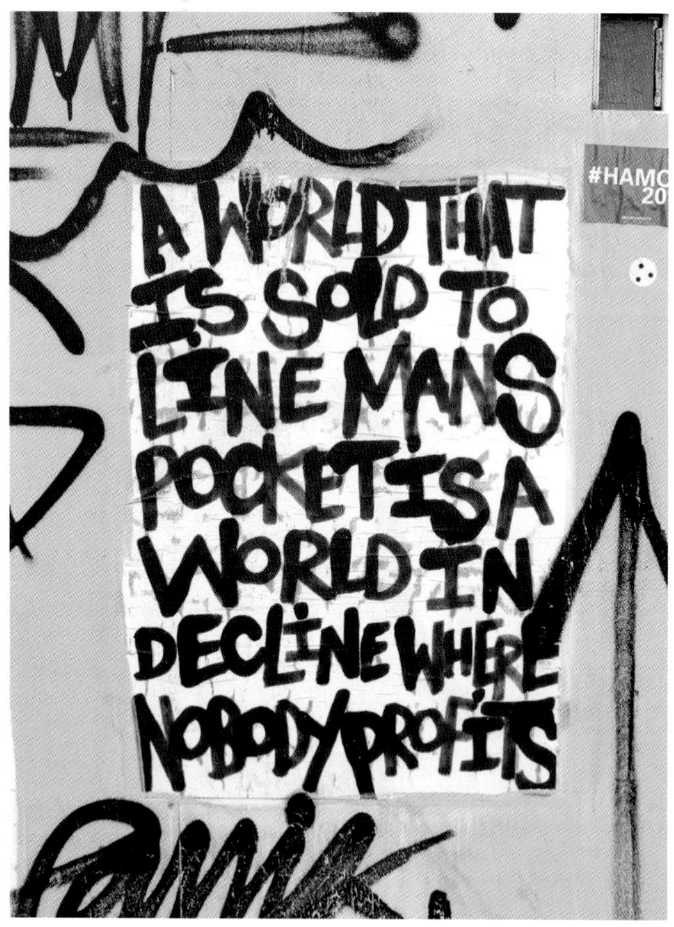
A WORLD THAT
IS SOLD TO
LINE MANS
POCKET IS A
WORLD IN
DECLINE WHERE
NOBODY PROFITS

2017: A world that is sold to line mans pocket is a world in decline where nobody profits

WHEREVER YOU GO, WHATEVER YOU DO, WHOEVER YOU ARE,
YOU ARE UNDER SURVEILLANCE
BECAUSE YOU ARE A POTENTIAL CRIMINAL. PERHAPS YOU SECRETLY DOUBT THE SANCTITY OF CORPORATE PROPERTY, OR THE VALIDITY OF LAWS MADE BY THE RICH TO GOVERN THE POOR, OR THE SOUNDNESS OF CAPITALISM ITSELF—WE CAN'T AFFORD TO ASSUME YOU DON'T. THAT'S WHY THERE ARE VIDEO CAMERAS POINTED AT EVERY CASHIER AND POLICE CARS CIRCLING EVERY BLOCK. LEFT TO ITSELF, A STATE OF DISORDER AND INEQUITY RETURNS TO EQUILIBRIUM; OUR JOB IS TO PERPETUATE THIS ONE INDEFINITELY.
C.C.TV. - Capitalist Control TV
Keeping you in fear of your lives

2011: You are under surveillance

2015: Holy Shit Bloody Corrupt [HSBC bank. Allegations were made that the bank had profited from doing business with corrupt politicians, dictators, tax evaders, arms dealers etc. Source: Wikipedia]

THE ONLY BANK THAT
GIVES YOU £5 EACH MONTH
GAVE £2·86 MILLION BONUS TO BANK BOSS
Switch to the Halifax Reward Current Account
Just pay in £1,000 each month.
JCDecaux

RESISTING SHELL
THE STRUGGLE AGAINST SHELLS CONTROVERSIAL CORRIB GAS PROJECT IN IRELAND CONTINUES, AND IS CURRENTLY ESCALATING IN RESPONSE TO SHELL BEGINNING WORK ON THE PROPOSED PIPELINE...
SCREENING OF 'THE PIPE' DOCUMENTARY FOLLOWED BY A Q+A+INFO SESSION ON THE CORRIB GAS PROJECT & ROSSPORT SOLIDARITY CAMP...
THE FACTORY*, APRIL TUES 12th, AFTER PEOPLES KITCHEN (... AROUND 8ISH)

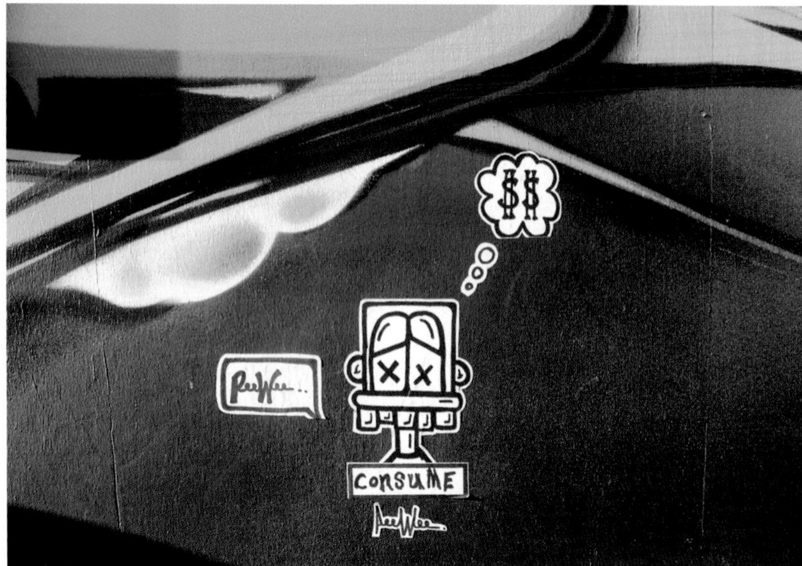

$$
CONSUME

Cops are not the sons of the workers...
...They are the dogs of the bosses

All 2011. Clockwise from top left - The only bank that gave £2.86 million bonus to bank boss | Resisting Shell | Cops are not the sons of the workers... they are the dogs of the bosses | PeeWee... consume |

Capitalism...

2011: I spy with my little eye... McPuke...

ENVIRONMENT...

We need a fundamental shift in our value systems, in order to bring ecological imperatives to the centre of our commerce and our actions.

Otherwise we're risking our collective future through the adverse effects of climate change (habitat destruction and species loss, water shortages, rising sea levels, desertification, spread of disease, disruption of climactic balance, mass migrations and conflict) as well as pollution and overconsumption.

World Bank chief economist Nicholas Stern, author of the Stern Review on the economics of climate change, describes the changes now under way in Earth's atmosphere as "the greatest and widest-ranging market failure ever seen."

"We should be practising a sustainable approach to economics that takes advantage of the ability of markets to allocate scarce resources while explicitly recognizing that our economy is dependent on the broader ecosystem that contains it."

Worldwatch Institute president Christopher Flavin

We're finding out just how smart and adaptable we really are, but time is not on our side.

-ENRICH·NOT·EXPLOIT-
gnodal
BIOINDUCTION

CAPITALISM
VS.
THE CLIMATE
SYSTEM CHANGE
NOT
CLIMATE CHANGE

ENDANGERING THE
ENVIRONMENT
STOP
TTIP

NO FRACKING

Clockwise from top left - 2016: Enrich not exploit | 2015: Capitalism vs. the climate | 2014: No fracking way! | 2015: Endangering the environment. Stop TTIP |

Monsanto
CLOSED

2010: Monsanto

STEPHEN LAWRENCE
BOURNEMOUTH 99
SOMETHING SCARY IN THE DAIRY...
GENETICALLY MODIFIED ANIMAL FEED
GMOoooooo!
THERE IS NO REGULATION, NO RESEARCH AND NO CHOICE
Over half of Britain's milk, butter, cheese, meat
contaminated animal feed, and there is NO
Government - where's our choice now??
National GMO Rally & Carnival Procession
Fancy dress, pantomime cows, entertainments, and speakers.
Sunday 26th September 1999
FIRST DAY OF LABOUR PARTY CONFERENCE
Assemble 2pm Meyrick Park, Bournemouth
Procession to sea front and Labour Party Conference.
SAY NO TO GMO
COACHES FROM VARIOUS PARTS OF THE UK
DANCE MUSIC

1999: Something scary in the dairy, GMOOOooo

[Monsanto's development and marketing of genetically engineered seed and bovine growth hormone, as well as its aggressive litigation, political lobbying practices, seed commercialization practices and "strong-arming" of the seed industry have made the company controversial around the world]

Source: Wikipedia

Environment...

ONE PLANET. ONE CHANCE

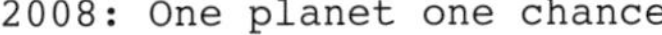
2008: One planet one chance

GLOBAL
WARMING
IS YOUR
FAULT

2008: Global warming is your fault

The evolution of POLLUTION
LET'S GO TO WORK
The new
arrived.
Commercial Vehicles
primesight

2010: The evolution of pollution

WARNING: This vehicle emits carbon dioxide,
carbon monoxide, nitrogen oxides, sulphur dioxide,
hydrocarbons, benzene, methane, aldehydes and VOCs.
Causes respiratory disease, cancer, death and ecocide.
ESPECIALLY HARMFUL TO OTHER SPECIES AND CHILDREN.

2007: Warning: This vehicle emits carbon dioxide…

Solar Panels
are
Industrial Installations. They
do not belong in the
COUNTRYSIDE

Westmark in association with Darfen helping to protect the environment.

THE 70 YR OLD PLANE TREE THAT ONCE STOOD HERE WOULD DISAGREE...

ecohoard

Win tickets to London 2012
with EDF Energy.
BOYCOTT EDF! NO TO NEW NUCLEAR BULLSHIT
WASTE ONLY
GENERAL WASTE ONLY

TOO BIG
TOO CLOSE
www.burtonjoyceparishcouncil.org.uk
www.re-volt.org.uk

Clockwise from top left - 2013: Solar Panels are Industrial Installations | 2009: The 70 yr old plane tree that once stood here would disagree... | 2012: Too big, too close [www.burtonjoyceparishcouncil.org.uk, www.re-volt.org.uk] | 2011: Boycott EDF! No to new nuclear bullshit |

Environment...

NOW U SEE ME,
SOON U WONT!
Seriously Thou!
IF WE DIE,
YOUR COMING WITH US x

2017: Now you see me, soon you wont!

TELL BRISTOL COUNCIL:
DON'T SPRAY POISON ON OUR STREETS
Bristol City Council are spraying toxic pesticides - likely to cause cancer - all over our streets and parks
WELCOME TO BRISTOL
38 DEGREES
Tell the Council that the people of Bristol refuse to be exposed to these chemicals any longer. Sign the petition:
ttps://secure.38degrees.org.uk/bristol-glyphosates-petition

2016: Tell Bristol Council don't spray poison on our streets

ONE LOVE
"MAJA"
OVER 100 MILLION YEARS ON EARTH,
BUT THE TURTLES TIME IS RUNNING OUT!

2016: Over 100 million years on earth

PANGOLIN - THE MOST
TRAFFICKED MAMMAL
IN THE WORLD!
ONE
BABA GANOUSH
FRESH COFFEE & JUICE BAR
MORNING MUNCH · RESTAURANT · BYO

2015: Pangolin – the most trafficked mammal in the world!

LEFT AND RIGHT...

GYMRU
Earth's Most Endangered Species:
THE WHITE RACE!
Help preserve it!
www.panzerfaust.com
MAX PENALT

HOME
WHITE POWER!
WE MUST SECURE THE EXISTENCE OF OUR RACE...
... AND A FUTURE FOR WHITE CHILDREN!
www.politicalsoldier.net
WCH

WHITE PEOPLE!
WHO SPEAKS FOR YOU?
WE DO!
www.england-first.org
Tel: 0121 241 7916
e-mail: info@england-first.org

SAY N
unlimited
migratio
our borders
RACIST
TO HELP CALL FREE 0800 587 6 587 or visit ukip.org
UKIP
TITAN

Above. Clockwise from top left - 2004: Earth's most endangered species [www.panzerfaust.com] | 2004: White power [www.politicalsoldier.net] | 2009: Say no to unlimited immigration [UKIP] | 2004: White people who speaks for you [www.england-first.org] |

Right. Clockwise from top left – 2004: Remember Toussaint L'Ouverture another world is possible [black leader of Haitian revolution in the 1790s] | 2004: There's only one solution - revolution | 2007: Working class power | 2004: Revolution is the locomotive of history | 2007: Another world is possible | 2008: Paris May 1968 [student protests, general strike, revolution in the air] |

REMEMBER TOUSSAINT L'OUVERTURE
ANOTHER WORLD IS POSSIBLE

THERE'S ONLY ONE
SOLUTION–REVOLUTION

PARIS MAY 1968

WORKING
CLASS
POWER

ANOTHER
WORLD IS
POSSIBLE

REVOLUTION IS THE LOCOMOTIVE OF HISTORY

NO TO THE BNP
HITLER'S SPAWN
primesight

2010: No to the BNP, Hitler's spawn

Left and right...

FACISTS RACISTS
HATERS OF REFUGEES
FOLLOW YOUR
LEADER

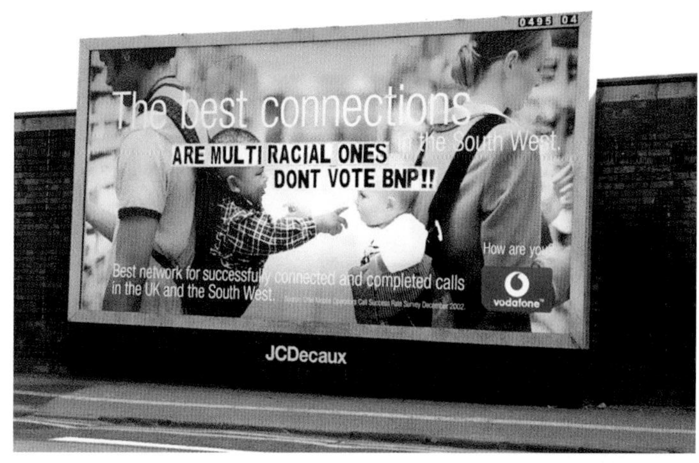
The best connections
in the South West.
ARE MULTI RACIAL ONES
DONT VOTE BNP!!
Best network for successfully connected and completed calls
in the UK and the South West.
How are you
vodafone
JCDecaux

BRISTOL RESISTANCE
MY GRANDAD FOUGHT HITLER -
I'M FIGHTING
THE BNP!
http://bristolresistance.blogspot.com

NO BNP
STUFF
THANKS

Clockwise from top left - 2007: Facists racists haters of refugees follow your leader | 2003: The best connections are multiracial ones, don't vote BNP | 2009: No BNP stuff thanks | 2010: Bristol Resistance my grandad fought Hitler |

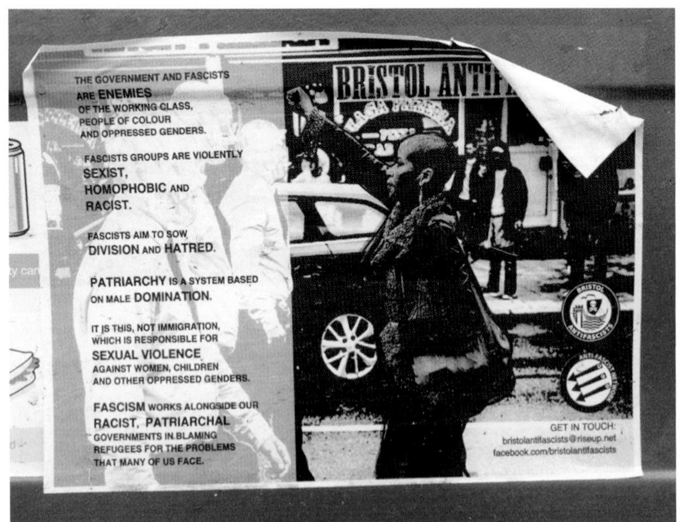
THE GOVERNMENT AND FASCISTS ARE ENEMIES OF THE WORKING CLASS, PEOPLE OF COLOUR AND OPPRESSED GENDERS.
FASCISTS GROUPS ARE VIOLENTLY SEXIST, HOMOPHOBIC AND RACIST.
FASCISTS AIM TO SOW DIVISION AND HATRED.
PATRIARCHY IS A SYSTEM BASED ON MALE DOMINATION.
IT IS THIS, NOT IMMIGRATION, WHICH IS RESPONSIBLE FOR SEXUAL VIOLENCE AGAINST WOMEN, CHILDREN AND OTHER OPPRESSED GENDERS.
FASCISM WORKS ALONGSIDE OUR RACIST, PATRIARCHAL GOVERNMENTS IN BLAMING REFUGEES FOR THE PROBLEMS THAT MANY OF US FACE.
BRISTOL ANTIF
GET IN TOUCH:
bristolantifascists@riseup.net
facebook.com/bristolantifascists

PURE
GO D
BOB CROW
TONY BENN
CLEAR

The February Revolution: Lessons for Today
7th March / 6PM
The White Bear
133 St Michael's Hill,
Bristol - BS2 8BS
RCG
FRFI.CO.UK
BRISTOL RCG
HOSTED BY THE REVOLUTIONARY COMMUNIST GROUP BRISTOL

ENGLISH DEFENCE LEAGUE
ARE WELCOME IN BRISTOL ... DON'T LIKE IT? BUGGER OFF !!!
R st EDL
not welcome
in Bristol!
Celebrating diversity —
Resisting racism and fascism.
Saturday 14 July
Rally and March ● Assemble
11am, Fountains, Bristol City Centre
Called by We Are Bristol supported by Unite Against Fascism

Clockwise from top left - 2017: Bristol Antifascists [bristolantifascists@riseup.net] | 2014: Pure gold – Bob Crow, Tony Benn [RMT (Rail Maritime and Transport) union leader Bob Crow died in March 2014] | 2012: English Defence League rally and march | 2017: The February Revolution – Lessons for Today [The first of two revolutions in Russia in 1917. Meeting hosted by the Bristol Revolutionary Communist Group] |

0003 01
Our
future.
It's in
our hands.
SUPPORT THE
POSTAL WORKERS
Overcome
work challenges
VICTORY TO THEPOSTAL WORKERS
skills.
visit lsc.gov.uk/inourhan
TITAN

2007: Support the postal workers

RICH AND POOR...

The laws protect the Rich only
Remember
G20

Above - 2009: The laws protect the rich only

Right. Clockwise from top left - 2006: Evict the rich | 2008: The rich only sleep at night because we let 'em | 2004: No more inheriteted wealth | 2004: It costs more to be poor | 2004: Make poverty and that lerricomtwang Geldof history [Bob Geldof was behind Band Aid and Live Aid raising money for poverty-stricken African countries] | 2011: The poor they rob with a pistol |

"EVICT THE RICH"
'AND EAT THE
OVERFED BASTARDS'

BASH THE RICH.
THE RICH ONLY
SLEEP AT
NIGHT
BECAUSE
WE LET
'EM...

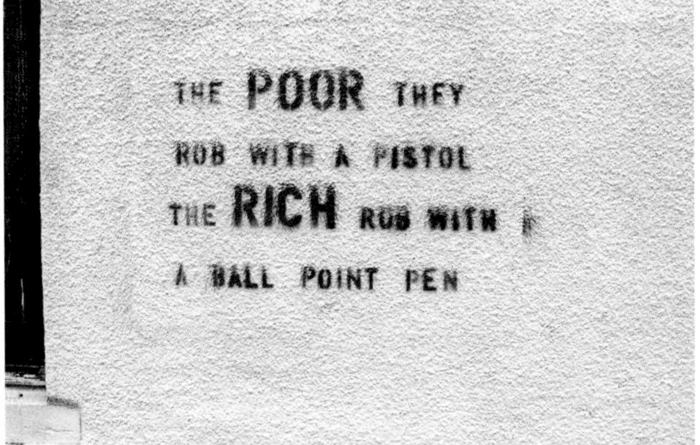
THE POOR THEY
ROB WITH A PISTOL
THE RICH ROB WITH
A BALL POINT PEN

NO MORE INHERITETED
WEALTH

ALL the goodness of wholegrain...
MAKE POVERTY AND
THAT LERRICOMTWANG GELDOF HISTORY
Weetos
Alpen
Weetabix
Weetaflakes
Weetabix Minis
Ready brek
What are you made of?
JCDecaux

IT COSTS
MORE TO
BE POOR

You'll need every minute
of your lunch hour
TO FIGHT FOR A DECENT WAGE
primesight

MORE
CHANCES TO
BECOME A
MILLIONAIRE
#PLEASENOTTHEM
IF YOU ARE A TORY MP
primesight

WE SENTENCE YOU TO DEBT
primesight

ETON
POSSE
HOAX
workshop 22

Clockwise from top left - 2015: You'll need every minute of your lunch hour | 2015: More chances to become a millionaire | 2012: Eton posse [Boris Johnson and David Cameron were educated at Eton. As were 1 in 10 of the MPs elected in 2017] | 2011: We sentence you to debt |

Rich and poor...

0495 01
THE NEW NISSAN PATHFINDER
IF SHIT WAS GOLD THEPOOR WOULDN'T BE
ALLOWED ARSEHOLES
PATHFINDER
MORE POWER, BIGGER SPACE, BETTER STORIES
NISSAN
JCDecaux

2004: If shit was gold the poor wouldn't be allowed arseholes

RACISM...

BLACK LIVES MATTER
NO STREET DRINKING ZONE
LOVE

2016: Black Lives Matter

PUBLIC RALLY – ALL WELCOME!
BRISTOL STANDS UP TO RACISM
• Refugees and migrants welcome here
• No to racism, Islamophobia & antisemitism
• Defend EU workers
• Black Lives Matter
Thursday 9 February, 7.15pm
Broadmead Baptist Church, Union Street, Bristol, BS1 3HY
Speakers:
Moazzam Begg
CAGE outreach director and former Guantanamo Bay detainee
Hibaq Jama
Labour councillor for Lawrence Hill
Terry Karampini
EU migrant worker and "One Day Without Us" activist
Weyman Bennett & Nahella Ashraf
Stand Up To Racism

2017: Bristol stands up to racism

SHOP/CONSUME...

Socrates (c.470 BC – 399 BC): "How many things I have no need of"

YOU NEED MORE STUFF.
primesight

2010: You need more stuff

TESCO
Very little help

She's Faking it!
Work. Buy. Consume. Die.

JD
#1 for
Sweat Shop Labour.
help propagate poverty.
Buy our plastic shoes.
(the WTO will thank you!)
NIKE BENASSI
ADIDAS PHOAX
QUICKSILVER RETRO SERIES

IKEA
MUST
BURN

40,312 POSSIBLE COMBINATIONS.
& ALL CRAP!
The new McChoice menu. 99p each.

FLY LESS
BUY LESS
LIVE MORE
CONSUMER OR
PARTICIPANT ?

BUY ✓
Think X

THINKLOCAL
TESCO

More reasons to shop at
BUYCOT SUPERMARKETS & THIER
POISONS AND BUY ORGANIC.
MORRISONS

Top row from left - 2011: Tesco. Very little help | 2002: She's faking it! Work. Buy. Consume. Die. | 2005: JD #1 for sweatshop labour | Middle row - 2001: Ikea must burn | 2002: 40,312 combinations & all crap! | 2017: Fly less, buy less, live more. Consumer or participant? | Bottom row - 2002: Buy think | 2010: Think local no Tesco | 2005: Buycot supermarkets & thier poisons and buy organic |

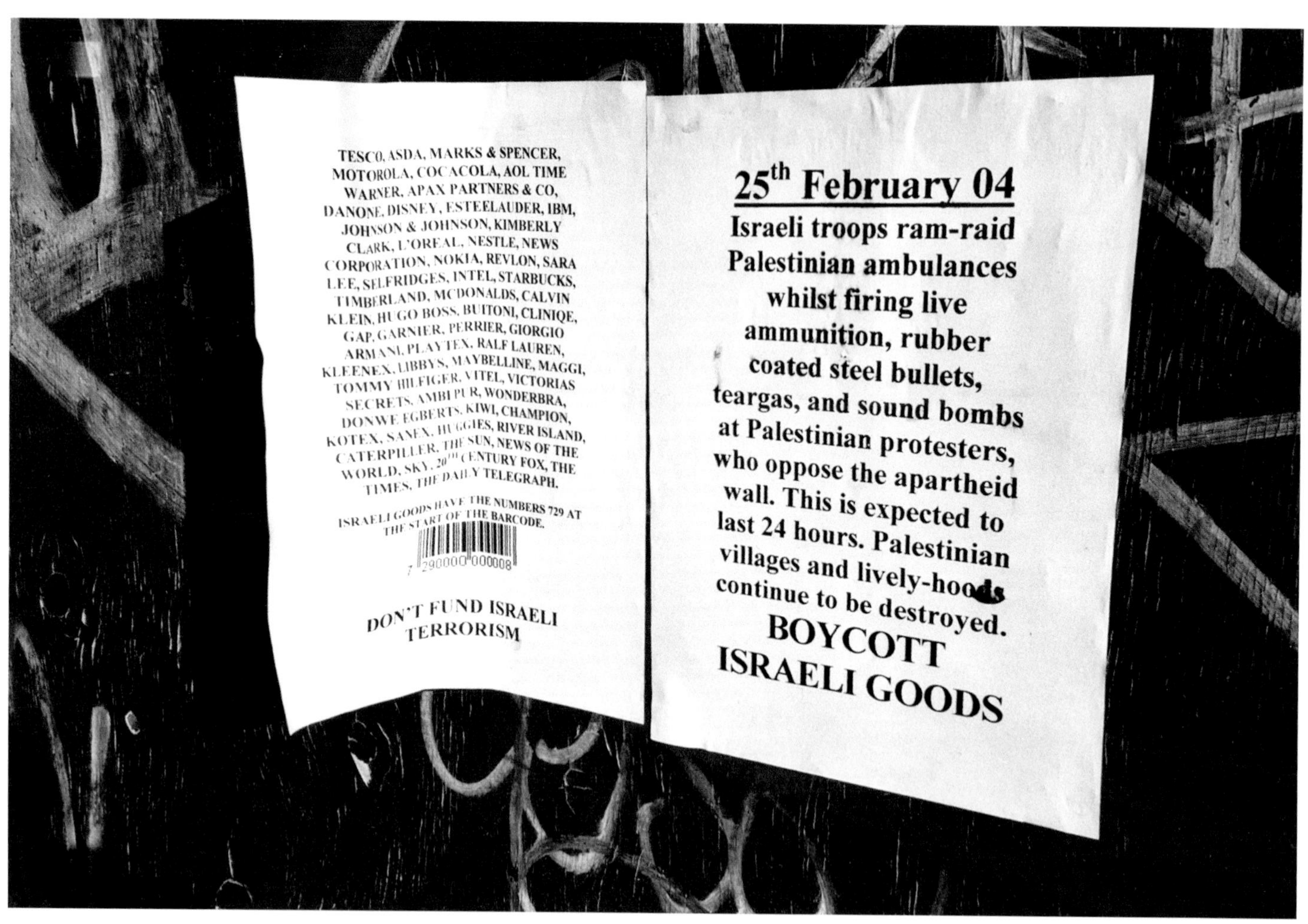
TESCO, ASDA, MARKS & SPENCER, MOTOROLA, COCACOLA, AOL TIME WARNER, APAX PARTNERS & CO, DANONE, DISNEY, ESTEELAUDER, IBM, JOHNSON & JOHNSON, KIMBERLY CLARK, L'OREAL, NESTLE, NEWS CORPORATION, NOKIA, REVLON, SARA LEE, SELFRIDGES, INTEL, STARBUCKS, TIMBERLAND, MCDONALDS, CALVIN KLEIN, HUGO BOSS, BUITONI, CLINIQE, GAP, GARNIER, PERRIER, GIORGIO ARMANI, PLAYTEX, RALF LAUREN, KLEENEX, LIBBYS, MAYBELLINE, MAGGI, TOMMY HILFIGER, VITEL, VICTORIAS SECRETS, AMBI PUR, WONDERBRA, DONWE EGBERTS, KIWI, CHAMPION, KOTEX, SANEX, HUGGIES, RIVER ISLAND, CATERPILLER, THE SUN, NEWS OF THE WORLD, SKY, 20TH CENTURY FOX, THE TIMES, THE DAILY TELEGRAPH.
ISRAELI GOODS HAVE THE NUMBERS 729 AT THE START OF THE BARCODE.
7 290000 000008
DON'T FUND ISRAELI TERRORISM
25th February 04
Israeli troops ram-raid Palestinian ambulances whilst firing live ammunition, rubber coated steel bullets, teargas, and sound bombs at Palestinian protesters, who oppose the apartheid wall. This is expected to last 24 hours. Palestinian villages and lively-hoods continue to be destroyed.
BOYCOTT ISRAELI GOODS

2004: Boycott Israeli goods

2006: Shit's all about you Nescafé. Screamin babies

[Nescafé's parent company Nestlé have been subject to boycotts since the 1970s, prompted by concern about the company's marketing of breast milk substitutes (infant formula), particularly in less economically developed countries (LEDCs), which campaigners claim contributes to the unnecessary death and suffering of babies, largely among the poor]

Source: Wikipedia

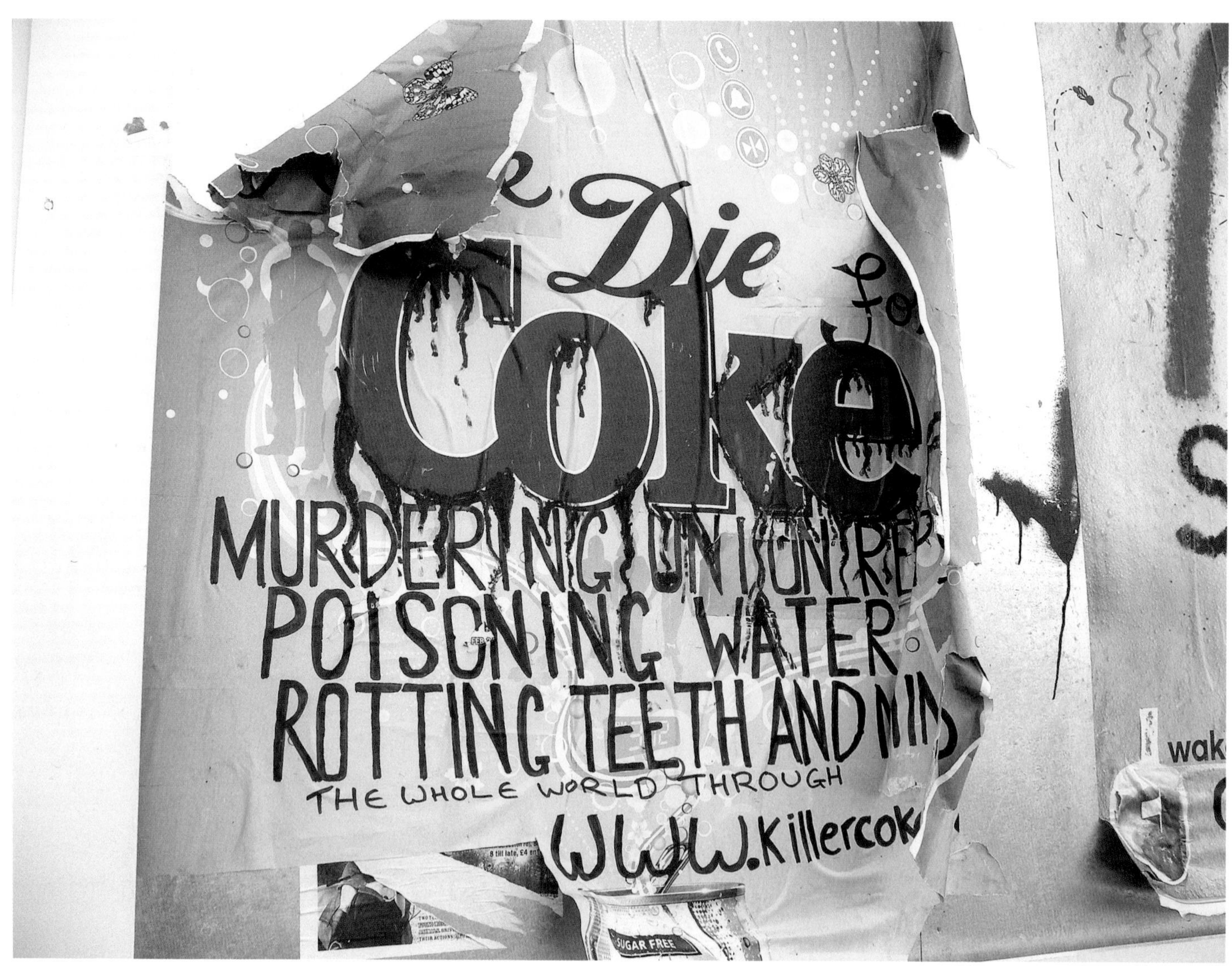
Die
Coke
MURDERING UNION REP
POISONING WATER
ROTTING TEETH AND MIN
THE WHOLE WORLD THROUGH
WWW.killercok
SUGAR FREE

2007: Die Coke [www.killercoke.org]

Shop/consume...

2007: McShite

93% OF LOCAL PeoPle SAY NO To TESCO!!
THINK LOCAL
NO TESCO
Our Council Must listen.
College Green Sept 22nd. 2pm.
Make your voice count.
NOTESCOINSTOKESCROFT.ORG.UK
RIOT
SOFA RIOT
NO STREET DRINKING ZONE

2010: Think local no Tesco [www.notescoinstokescroft.org.uk]

2010: No Tesco in Stokes Croft

HOUSING...

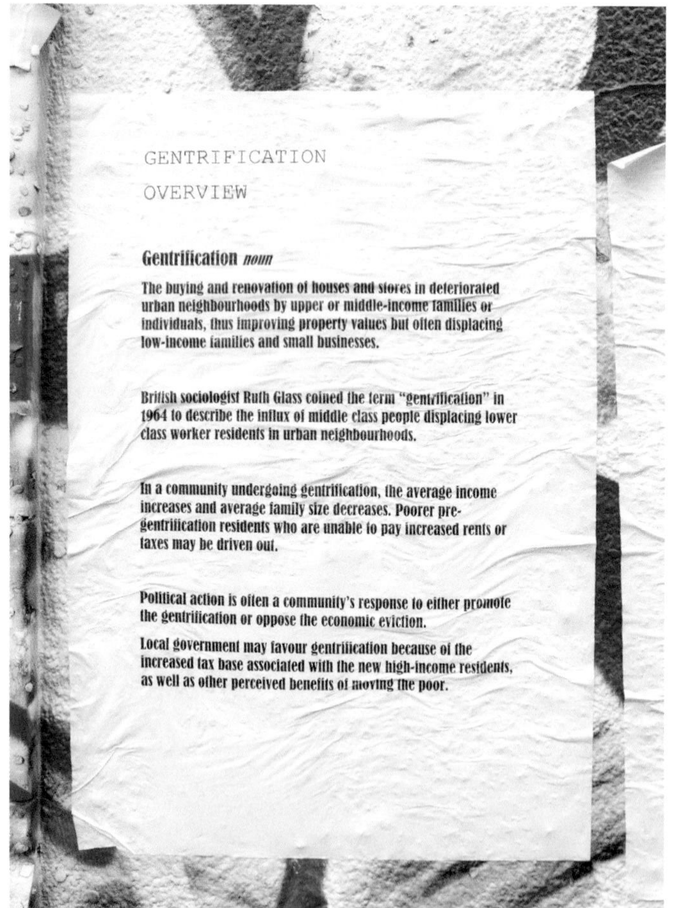
GENTRIFICATION
OVERVIEW
Gentrification noun
The buying and renovation of houses and stores in deteriorated urban neighbourhoods by upper or middle-income families or individuals, thus improving property values but often displacing low-income families and small businesses.
British sociologist Ruth Glass coined the term "gentrification" in 1964 to describe the influx of middle class people displacing lower class worker residents in urban neighbourhoods.
In a community undergoing gentrification, the average income increases and average family size decreases. Poorer pre-gentrification residents who are unable to pay increased rents or taxes may be driven out.
Political action is often a community's response to either promote the gentrification or oppose the economic eviction.
Local government may favour gentrification because of the increased tax base associated with the new high-income residents, as well as other perceived benefits of moving the poor.

2013: Gentrification overview

SUPPORT
for
ROUGH SLEEPERS
NEED SOMEWHERE TO STAY?
The Compass Centre can provide somewhere to live as well as healthcare and training. Call them on:
0117 944 0581
or visit: The Compass Centre
Jamaica Street
St Pauls
Bristol BS2 8JP
HELP WITH DRUGS
You can get help and advice from Bristol Drugs Project. Call them on:
0117 987 600
or visit: Bristol Drugs Project
11 Brunswick Square
BS2 8PE
TOILETS
Nearby in Wetherspoons, Colston Hall and Castle Park.

2016: Support for rough sleepers

MORTGAGES
Nationwide
1 in 3 people are paying too much for their mortgage
Be different - switch to Nationwide
SQUATTING STILL LEGAL
Nationwide Underlining the difference
www.nationwide.co.uk
0800 30 20 10
or visit us today
Banking
Credit Card
Insurance
Investments
Loans
Mortgages
Pensions
Savings

PAINTWORKS UNLEASHED
Crest
A UNIQUE DEVELOPMENT OF ONE + TWO BEDROOM APARTMENTS, TWO, THREE + FOUR BED HOUSES AND LIVE/WORK UNITS
REGISTER TODAY
COUNCIL HOUSES UNBUILT
primesight

WOT NO CHEAP HOUSING?

Trouble with landlords?
Angry over thousands of empties?
DECENT HOMES FOR ALL
- fight every eviction threat
let's create local solidarity groups
to resist oppression & injustice
http://hsg.cupboard.org

Clockwise from top left - 2001: Squatting still legal | 2016: Council houses unbuilt [referencing Bristol Mayoral election pledges to build council houses] | 2009: Decent homes for all | 2005: Wot no cheap housing? |

WAR...

Since 2000 the UK has been involved in:

- Sierra Leone Civil War (2000)
- The 'War on Terror' (2001–present)
- The Afghanistan War (2001–2014)
- Iraq War (2003–2009)
- ISIL (2014-present)

Earlier conflicts:

- Northern Ireland Troubles (1969-mid 1990s)
- Cod War Confrontation (1975–1976)
- Falklands War (1982)
- The First Gulf War (1990–1991)
- The Bosnian War (1995–1996)
- The Kosovo War (1999)

Source: Wikipedia

Clockwise from top left – 2002: War means profit invest your sons | 2003: Democracy we deliver | 2003: Drop rhymes not bombs | 2008: Richmond Road against the war | 2010: Not in my name (Stop the War Coalition) [www.stopwar.org.uk]) | 2003: War sucks |

"WE SHALL NEITHER FAIL NOR FALTER;
WE SHALL NOT WEAKEN OR TIRE."
WINSTON CHURCHILL
WAR MEANS PROFIT INVEST YOUR SONS
LEGION
Playground

DEMOCRACY
WE DELIVER

WAR
SUCKS.

DROP
Rhymes = NOT BOMBS

NOT IN
MY NAME
Stop the War Coalition www.stopwar.org.uk 020 7053 2153/4/5/6

RICHMOND
ROAD
AGAINST
THE
WAR

elim@bristol
city church
Lifestyle
Centre
PRIVATE
No
Parking
W.M.I
WAR, WHAT IS IT GOOD FOR?
"BRUTALIZING THE MASSES SO THAT THEY ARE ALWAYS TOO TERRORIZED
TO NOTICE THE "REPTILLIAN AGENDA"/"NEW WORLD ORDER", UNFOLDING
AROUND THEM."

2002: War, what is it good for?

WE ARE ALL BRUTALISED BY CONFLICT
SUPPORTED THE WAR
STARTED THE WAR
SUPPORTS THE OCCUPATION
DON'T VOTE WAR
JCDecaux

2005: We are all brutalised by conflict - Don't vote war

[This billboard by GraphicAttack shows then Conservative leader Michael Howard, Labour's Tony Blair, and Liberal Democrat Charles Kennedy, two years after the invasion of Iraq]

RETURN TO AFGHANISTAN

AND BRING TROOPS HOME

ROSS KEMP GOES BACK TO THE F ONT LINE

FEB

sky1 HD

EXPERIENCE MORE IN HIGH DEFINITION

TITAN

FIGHT
WAR
NOT
WARS
WWW.ACTIVEDISTRIBUTION.ORG
WWW.CAAT.ORG.UK

Above - 2015: Fight war not wars [www. activedistribution.org, www.caat.org.uk]

Left - 2009: Return to Afghanistan and bring troops home [British troops were part of an International Security Assistance Force in Afghanistan since 2001. In 2014 combat operations ended but around 500 troops remained. In 2017 NATO requested more troops from the US and UK]

2003: No War

UK DUTY PAID
WARNING
Bombing women
during pregnancy
may harm their
unborn babies
A gHOSTbOY HEALTH WARNING

THE UN OBSERVERS
FAILED
THE WEAPONS OF
MASS DESTRUCTION WERE
HERE
sc*re

NO BLOOD FOR OIL
Don't BELIEVE BLAIR
JCDecaux

STOP
WARS

All 2003: Clockwise from top left - Bombing women during pregnancy may harm their unborn babies (a gHOSTbOY health warning) | UN observers failed - the weapons of mass destruction were here | Stop Wars | No blood for oil - don't believe Blair |

REFUGEES AND MIGRANTS...

BRISTOL'S
BEATING
HEART
colstonhall.org
REFUGEES WELCOME
primesight

2015: Refugees welcome

2016: We are all immigrants

LOVE
JUSTICE
for REFUGEES and
MIGRANTS stuck in
the Calais and Dunkirk
'jungles'!
JUSTICE FOR REFUGEES ON FRENCH-UK BORDERS

2016: Justice for refugees and migrants

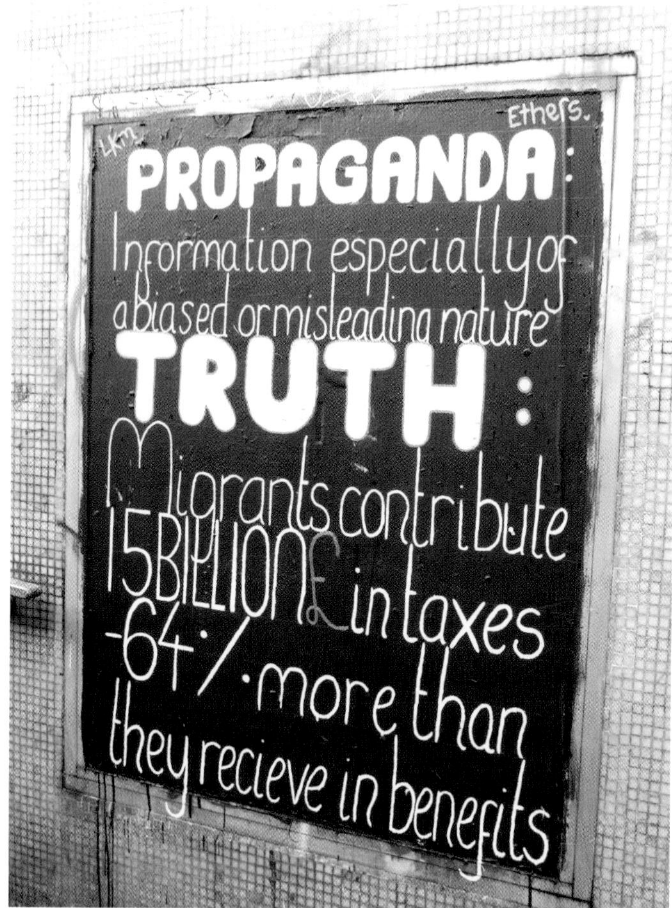
Ethers.
PROPAGANDA:
Information especially of
a biased or misleading nature
TRUTH:
Migrants contribute
15BILLION£ in taxes
-64% more than
they recieve in benefits

2015: Propaganda & truth

Next page clockwise from top left - 2016: Enough money and space | 2013: If it were not for migration then where would we be? | 2015: Find your beach awash with corpses [more than 1000 refugees drowned in the Mediterranean from January to April 2017. Hundreds wash up on beaches] | 2014: Support for LGBTQ asylum seekers | 2017: The Islamisation of Europe | 2007: Migration is not a crime |

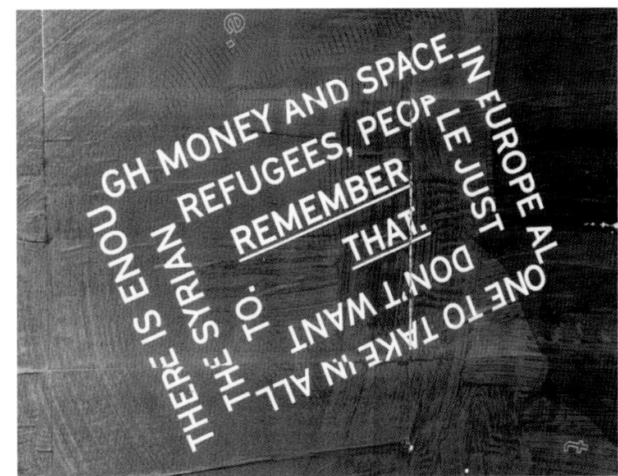
THERE IS ENOUGH MONEY AND SPACE IN EUROPE ALONE TO TAKE IN ALL
THE SYRIAN REFUGEES, PEOPLE JUST DON'T WANT
TO. REMEMBER THAT.

IF IT WERE NOT FOR
MIGRATION
THEN WHERE WOULD WE BE?

MIGRATION
IS NOT A CRIME

Find your beach.
Corona Extra
AWASH WITH CORPSES
JCDecaux

ISLAMISATION
THE OF EUROPE
HAPPENING UNDER OUR NOSES!
LETS CLOSE OUR
BORDERS!!

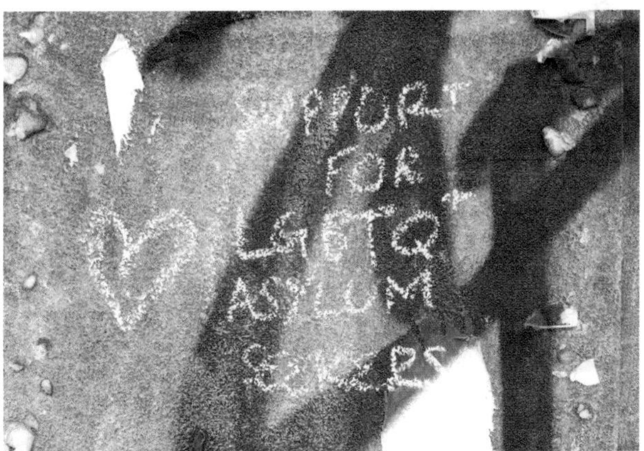
SUPPORT
FOR
LGBTQ+
ASYLUM
SEEKERS

BILLBOARDS AND ADVERTISING...

POPSTARS
SUBVERTISE
We all find strength in something.

2001: Subvertise

SOAPY & FRITZ SAY NO MORE ADVERTS.
More O'Ferrall

2001: Soapy & Fritz say no more adverts

IF BRITAIN WERE FRENCH...
THIS POSTER
WOULDN'T BE CENSORED.
IF BRITAIN WERE ENLIGHTENED...
THIS WOMAN
WOULDN'T BE EXPLOITED

2002: If Britain were enlightened... this woman wouldn't be exploited

RENAULT MEGANE
NOT JUST
A PRETTY
BOTTOM
CRAP AD OF THE YEAR
RENAULT
JCDecaux
BT

2006: Crap ad of the year

049501
IMAGINE A

049502
WORLD WITHOUT
049503
BILLBOARDS

talk for free
talk.
THIS AD HAS BEEN CANCELLED FOR
YOUR PSYCHOLOGICAL PROTECTION
from THE Carphone Warehouse
000.

2004: This ad has been cancelled for your psychological protection

AGGON &
HORSES
MP 124601
DON'T JUST SHAVE
SECONDS
OFF YOUR BEST TIME.
TAKE A CHAINSAW TO IT !!
DESTROY MORE BILLBOARDS
Have you got
score outdoor

2001: Destroy more billboards

WOMEN...

2016: Gender equality

"FIGHT SEXISM"

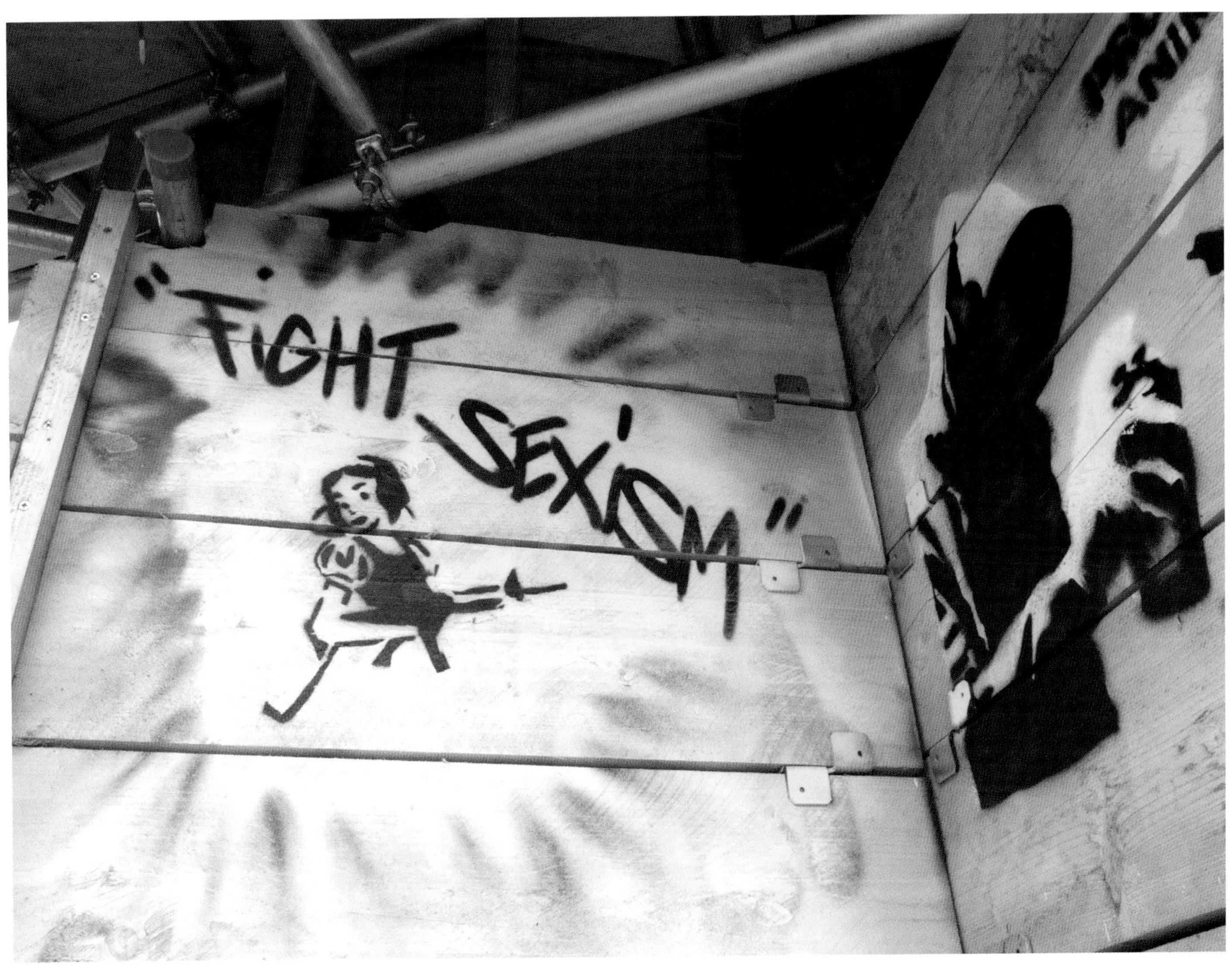

2017: Fight sexism

MY OUTFIT
IS NOT AN
INVITATION
Stoptellingwomentosmile.com

2016: My outfit is not an invitation
[stoptellingwomentosmile.com]

A SISTERS UNCUT GUIDE TO
TAKING
ACTION
LISTEN
TAKE THE LEAD FROM THOSE AFFECTED. SURVIVORS, SERVICE USERS, SECTOR WORKERS.
RESEARCH
USE LOCAL KNOWLEDGE. SOLID STATISTICS ARE GREAT.
SOLIDARITY - NETWORK
ARE WE ORGANISING INTERSECTIONALLY? LINK UP. FEMINIST, MIGRANT SOLIDARITY, HOUSING, ANTI CUTS, LGBTQ GROUPS...
LOGISTICS
WORK OUT A PLAN OF ACTION.
ACCESS
ACCESS TEAM
AS FAR AS POSSIBLE, MAKE THE SPACE SAFE FOR SISTERS.
PROPAGANDA
2 WOMEN A WEEK
THEY CUT WE BLEED
MAKE ACTIONS LOOK STRIKING.
MEDIA
GET THE MESSAGE OUT.
PLANNING
KEY MESSAGES
2
WOMEN A WEEK KILLED BY A PARTNER OR EX-PARTNER IN THE UK
STOP
CUTS TO DOMESTIC VIOLENCE SERVICES
MAKE THEM CLEAR.
TAKE ACTION
SISTERS! UNITED! WILL NEVER BE DEFEATED!
MAKE SURE SISTERS ARE BRIEFED ON THEIR LEGAL RIGHTS.
BE FRIENDLY AND SUPPORTIVE TO NEW SISTERS.
HAVE SPECIFIC GROUPS OF SISTERS MAKING SURE EVERYONE IS OKAY.
TELL THE WORLD
NEWS
BREAKING
- DEBRIEF - REFLECT -
- SUPPORT - GROW -
IT IS OUR DUTY TO FIGHT FOR OUR FREEDOM.
IT IS OUR DUTY TO WIN.
WE MUST LOVE AND SUPPORT ONE ANOTHER.
WE HAVE NOTHING TO LOSE BUT OUR CHAINS.
- ASSATA SHAKUR
WWW.SISTERSUNCUT.ORG
@SISTERSUNCUT

2017: Sisters uncut guide to taking action
[www.sistersuncut.org]

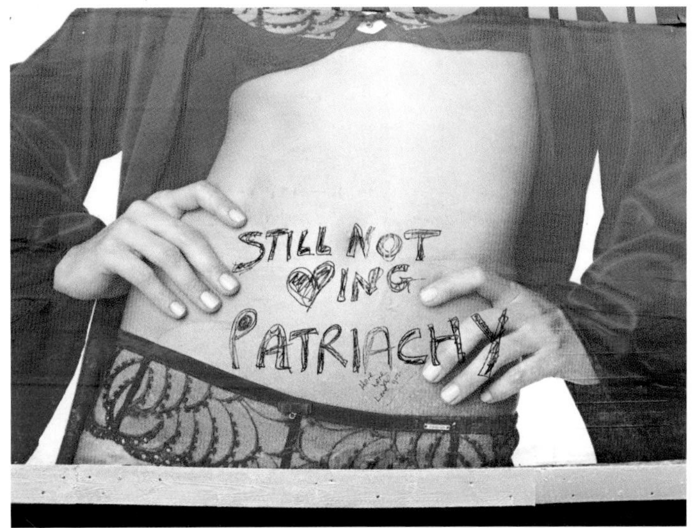
STILL NOT
♥ING
PATRIACHY

LADYFEST
B*A*S*H
RECLAIM THE PATH
HI VIS MARCH
FIND US FROM 5-7PM
NEXT TO THE CYCLE PATH
9TH OCTOBER MARCH STARTS AT 7PM

Women! unite! You hold The power of creation!
Stop Violence Against Women!
UniTeD in Love

MEN DO NOT OWN
THE STREETS
#STWTS
WOMEN
ARE NOT OUTSIDE FOR
YOUR ENTERTAINMENT
#STWTS
YOU ARE NOT
ENTITLED
TO MY BODY

Clockwise from top left - 2010: Still not loving patriachy | 2015: Reclaim The Path hi viz march | 2015: #stwts posters [stop telling women to smile] | 2013: Stop violence against women |

ANIMALS...

STOP THE OXFORD
ANIMAL
LAB

2006: Stop the Oxford Animal Lab

Next page. Clockwise from top left - 2002: Sunday morning worship we want blood | 2015: Save British wildlife cull Tories | 2016: household products, such as bleach are also tested on animals! | 2013: Murdered by Huntingdon Life Sciences [Europe's largest animal testing laboratory. www.shac.net] | 2007: Due to reckless deforestation | 2009: Meat kills. Go veggie [www.animalaid.org.uk] |

Sunday
morning
worship.
WE WANT
BLOOD.
Walls
MAIDEN

SAVE BRITISH
WILDLIFE
CULL TORIES
CULLTHETORIES.COM

MEAT KILLS
Go
Veggie
01732 364
www.animalaid.

HOUSEHOLD
PRODUCTS, SUCH AS
BLEACH ARE ALSO
TESTED ON
ANIMALS!

DUE TO...
1.RECKLESS
DEFORESTATION
2.POACHING
3.THE ILLEGAL
PET/ZOO TRADE
WILD ORANGUTANS
ARE DISAPPEARING
AT A RATE
5,000 PER YEAR

MURDERED
by HUNTINGDON LIFE SCIENCES
Life Sciences (HLS) are Europe's largest animal
laboratory, murdering 500 ca s, dogs, horses, monkeys
every single day. HLS have been exposed seven separate
for abusing primates, punching beagle puppies in the face
test data. Give them a call on: 01480 892000
shac.net

KEEP YOUR BULL****
IN WESTMINSTER
We'll keep ours in the countryside
JOIN US: call 01672 519490
www.countryside-alliance.org

2006: Keep your bull**** in Westminster [www.countryside-alliance.org]

FOX
OFF
BLAIR
BOLLOCKS
TO BLAIR
NO BAN

2004: Fox off Blair. Bollocks to Blair, No ban

[Location: South Wales valleys at the height of the debate on banning fox-hunting. Later in 2004 the ban became law]

CLASS WAR...

Class War is a UK class struggle based group and newspaper originally set up in 1983, subsequently mutating, disappearing and reviving by turns. Their uncompromisingly simple and insulting stickers make me smile.

TOFFS OUT!
CLASS UNITY
CLASS WAR
CLASS PRIDE
www.classwar.org

2010: Toffs out! [The image is from Ken Loach's 1969 film 'Kes']

CLASS UNITY
CLASS WAR
CLASS PRIDE
www.classwar.org
HURRY UP AND DIE
Party in Trafalgar Square
Saturday after Thatcher dies, 6pm

2010: Hurry up and die. Party in Trafalgar Square Saturday after [Margaret] Thatcher dies, 6pm

We still fucking hate
THATCHER!
CLASS WAR
PO Box 467, London E8 3QX www.classwar.org

DIFFERENT FACES
SAME SHIT
CLASS WAR
classwar-uk.blogspot.com

ALTERNATIVE ENERGY?
BURN THE RICH!
CLASS WAR
DIFFERENT FACES
SAME SHIT
CLASS WAR

PREACHERS?
BASTARDS!
CLASS WAR
PO Box 467, London E8 3QX www.classwar.org

POLITICIANS?
WANKERS!
CLASS WAR

MESS WITH OUR NHS
AND WE'LL MESS WITH YOU!
CLASS WAR
PO Box 467, London E8 3QX www.classwar.org

POP-EYED FASCISTS?
CLASS WAR
PO Box 467, London E8 3QX www.classwar.org

Bollocks To
The Countryside Alliance!
They Are Not Shagging Sheep
They Are Killing Foxes!
CLASS WAR

Capitalism
Is Killing
Football
CLASS WAR
PO BOX 467, London E8 3QX

Top row from left – 2008: We still fucking hate Thatcher! | 2014: Same faces different shit [Cameron and Thatcher] | 2010: Alternative energy? Burn the rich + Same faces different shit | Middle row from left - 2008: Preachers? Bastards! | 2009: Politicians? Wankers! | 2008: Mess with our NHS and we'll mess with you! | Bottom row from left - 2009: Popeyed fascists? Bastards [Nick Griffin, BNP] | 2007: Bollocks to the Countryside Alliance! When they are not shagging sheep they are killing foxes | 2006: Capitalism is killing football [Rupert Murdoch, owner of Sky TV] |

2007: Parasite! Class War [location: my local park]

Class War...

2007: Class [same sticker 2 months later]

BUSH AND BLAIR...

Imagine
getting RID OF BLAIR AND BUSH
:firstchoice.co.uk
Imagine your First Choice
Weight limit
Low bridge
100 yds ahead
7.5T
4.1m
13'-6"
JCDecaux

2004: Imagine getting rid of Blair and Bush

Right. Clockwise from top left – 2006: Liar liar knickers on fire | 2006: George Bush and Son. Family Butchers | 2003: Blood on your hands Mr Blair | 2009: Bye bye [George Bush left the White House in January 2009] | 2007: Last time in Chequers [Chequers is the country residence of the Prime Minister. Tony Blair was succeeded as PM by Gordon Brown in June 2007. He's wearing comic strip character Rupert the Bear's check trousers and scarf] | 2004: Deeply offended chimp |

LIAR
LIAR
KNICKERS
ON
FIRE

THE WARS
WILL BE OVER
WHEN THE POLITICIANS
GO TO FIGHT ON THE
FRONTLINE!
George Bush & Son
FAMILY BUTCHERS

DEEPLY OFFENDED CHIMP
STOP
THE
WAR

BLOOD
ON YOUR HANDS
MR BLAIR

LAST TIME
IN
CHEQUERS

CLEARCHANNEL
NOW AND THEN
The Legend's new TV show starts 10.20pm

2006: Now and then [Bush and Hitler replacing Terry Wogan in ad for the 'Wogan Now and Then' TV series]

Bush and Blair...

2002: The Clones

COWLIN CONSTRUCTION
BUSH
BLAIR
Evil never dies
PRESIDENT EVIL
IN CINEMAS JULY 12
www.residentevilthemovie.co.uk
Constantin Film
BT
What can BT do for y

2002: President Evil

Bush and Blair...

BUSH STINKS
OF BLOOD
AND BULLSHIT
(BLAIR TOO)
All I'm wearing. Now.
Video calls for the same price as voice.
3
CLEARCHANNEL

2003: Bush stinks of blood and bullshit (Blair too)

ARMS TRADE...

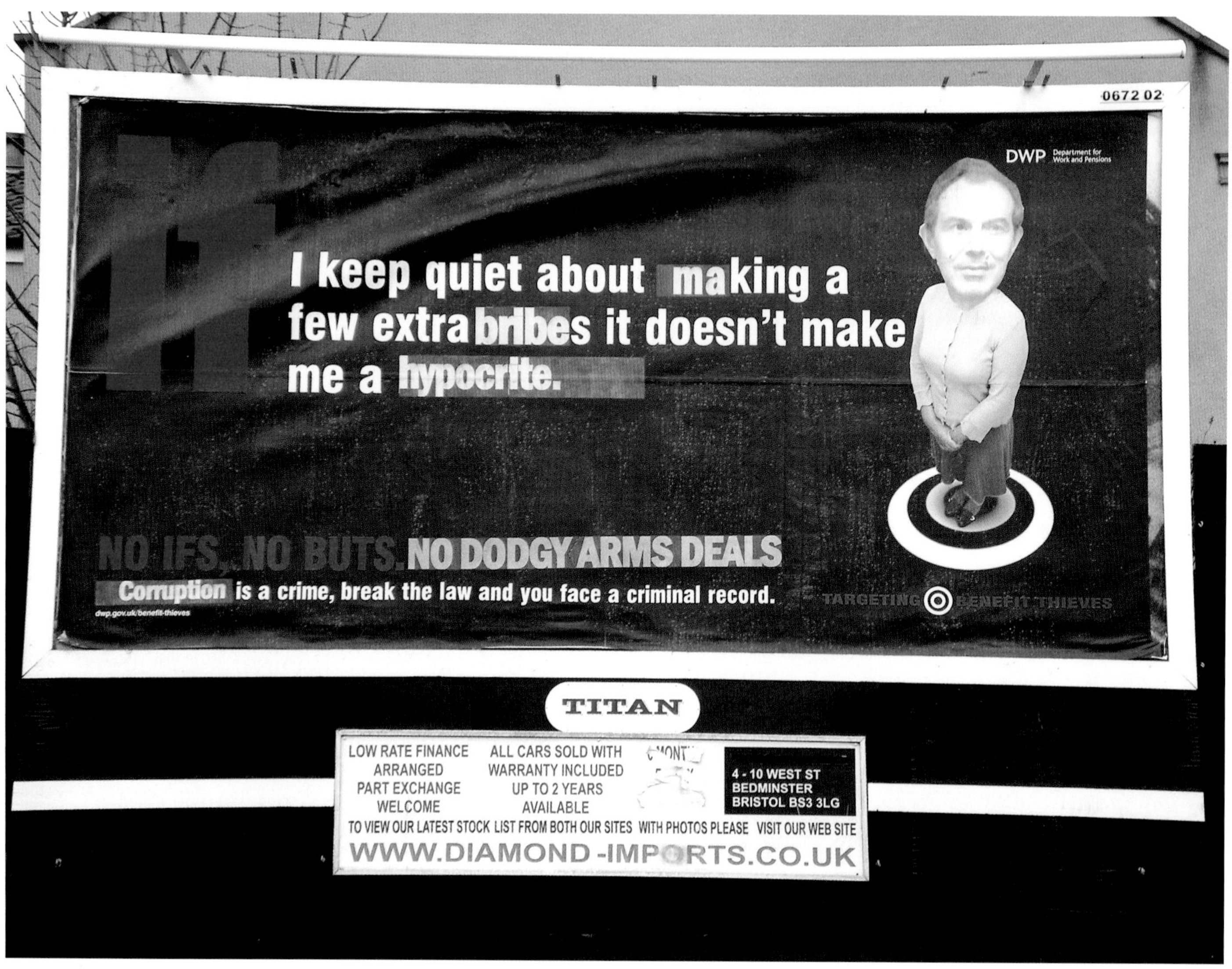
0672 02
DWP Department for Work and Pensions
If I keep quiet about making a few extra bribes it doesn't make me a hypocrite.
NO IFS, NO BUTS. NO DODGY ARMS DEALS
Corruption is a crime, break the law and you face a criminal record.
dwp.gov.uk/benefit-thieves
TARGETING BENEFIT THIEVES
TITAN
LOW RATE FINANCE ARRANGED PART EXCHANGE WELCOME
ALL CARS SOLD WITH WARRANTY INCLUDED UP TO 2 YEARS AVAILABLE
4 - 10 WEST ST BEDMINSTER BRISTOL BS3 3LG
TO VIEW OUR LATEST STOCK LIST FROM BOTH OUR SITES WITH PHOTOS PLEASE VISIT OUR WEB SITE
WWW.DIAMOND -IMPORTS.CO.UK

2006: If I keep quiet about making a few extra bribes

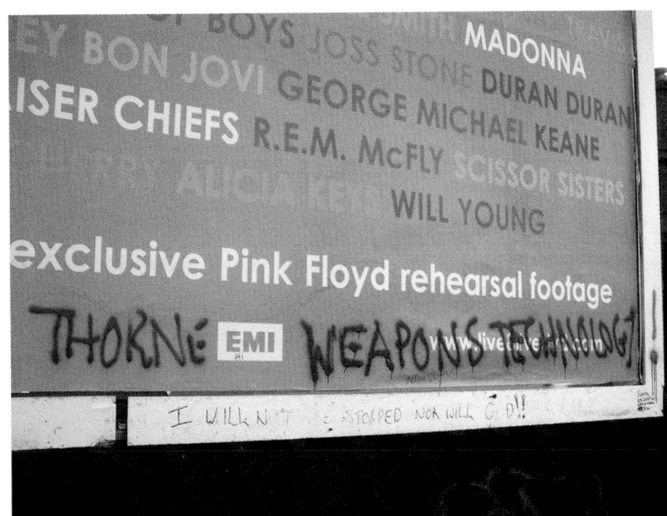

Clockwise from top left - 2010: Teachers not Trident | 2003: Multinationa£$ are making a killing out of our taxes | 2007: Royal International Air Tattoo, RAF Fairford [www.airtattoo.com] | 2005: Thorne EMI weapons technology [The EMI record label's association with weapons actually ended 10 years previously in 1995, when owners Thorn EMI sold its defence businesses] |

TEARS FOR THE FALLEN
ARMS THAT DO NOT HOLD + COMFORT
ARMS THAT MUTILATE + KILL
MADE IN BRISTOL

2017: Tears for the fallen

Arms Trade...

·ALL THE
ARMS WE
NEED·
E

2014: All the arms we need

DISARM DSEI 2009
12noon 8th September - City of London - Details TBC
DESTROY THE BANKS!
ESTROY THE INVESTORS!
ESTROY THE ARMS TRADE!
Systems Equipment International
- the world's largest arms fair - is
to take place in East London
8 and 11 September 2009.
info@dsei.org

2009: Disarm DSEI [A call to disrupt the Defence Systems Equipment International - the world's largest arms fair. www.dsei.org]

PALESTINE...

#FREE PALESTINE
STOP THE BLOODSHED!!
For more info Search for
-Bristol PSC
-Stop the War Coalition
-Breaking Silence
GRAFF 4
PALESTINE
on Fb

2014: Free Palestine. Stop the bloodshed!!

BOYCOTT
ISRAELI
GOODS
Free Palestine • www.palestinecampaign.org

STOP
APARTEID
IN
PALESTINE!

G4S HALT CHECKPOINT G4S
4 For ALL ISRAEL'S RACIST IDF
Security Jails for Palestinian KIDS
TORTURE CELLS. PLEASE STOP

BOYCOTT
ISRAELI
GOODS
Don't Squeeze a Jaffa
Crush the Occupation
FREE PALESTINE
http://www.palestinecampaign.org

Clockwise from top left - 2012: Boycott Israeli goods [www.palestinecampaign.org] | 2011: Stop aparteid in Palestine! | 2010: Don't squeeze a Jaffa, crush the occupation [www.palestinecampaign.org] | 2013: G4S [Private security firm G4S sold off its Israeli arm of the company in December 2016 after a campaign of boycotts and protests about human rights violations in border checkpoints and prisons] |

TRUMP...

A SPECIAL RELATIONSHIP

2017: A special relationship [Theresa May and Donald Trump]

2017: Captain America

2016: Fuck Trump

CARS...

Cars can have a symbolic quality – as classically capitalist in their appeal to our aspirations, and for their part in damaging our health and the environment. Billboards advertising cars are frequent targets.

It's estimated in 2014 that over 1.25 billion cars travel the streets and roads of the world today. They burn over 260 billion (US) gallons of petrol and diesel yearly (Source: Wikipedia).

They're inextricably integrated into national economies and personal lifestyles, and increasing in number year on year.

Leaving aside the amount of raw materials they require to manufacture, as long as they use fuel that is oil-based, cars are part of the problem.

4.1 m
13'-6"
CARRUPT

TITANIC
JCDecaux

Come rain
Come shine
20 ROAD DEATHS A DAY
VAUXHALL
JCDecaux

Attention
seeker
POLLUTION WREAKER
fiveyear
HYUNDAI

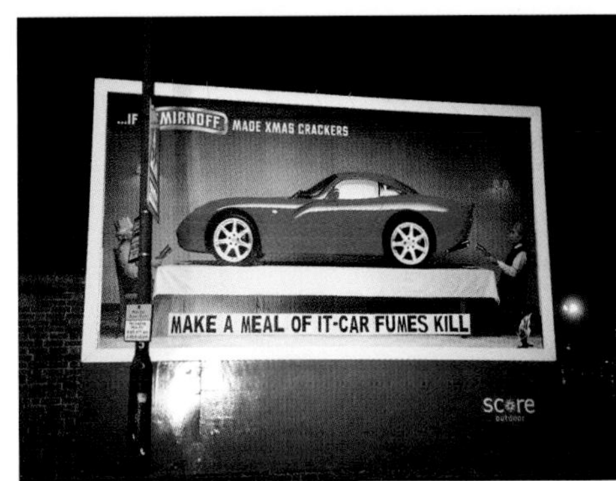
...IF MIRNOFF MADE XMAS CRACKERS
MAKE A MEAL OF IT-CAR FUMES KILL
score

Tollgate
Sat/Sun Parking
Park & Ride
It is big and it is clever
No it's NOT
FIAT
commercial vehicles

A NEW WAY TO LIVE FOR THE
21ST CENTURY
STOP
DRiving
BARRATT
the ZONE

0%ooh
VAT
WITH
APR
representative
On selected ŠKODAs
OR YOU Could RIDE
JCDecaux

www.theAA.com
There's no
courtesy car,
should I
walk ?-YES ?
YOU LAZY BASTARD

From top left - 2002: Carrupt | 2007: Titanic | 2006: 20 road deaths a day | Middle row - 2006: Attention seeker pollution wreaker | 2001: Make a meal of it - car fumes kill | 2002: No it's not | Bottom row - 2008: Stop driving | 2011: Or you could ride | 2003: There's no courtesy car, should I walk? Yes you lazy bastard |

IT'S QUICKER
BY BIKE!
Stress
Pol lution
congestion
Contact: Bristol Cycling Campaign EMAIL: BCCNEWS@gn.apc.org
Box 58 Greenleaf Bookshop 82 Colston St. BS1 5BB WWW.gn.apc.org/alt-transportbristol

1999: It's quicker by bike!

EXHILARATING PERFORMANCE WITH A CONSCIENCE.
LEXUS HYBRID DRIVE.
1224 01
BETTER TAKE THE BUS
www.lexus.co.uk
JCDecaux

2007: Better take the bus

2005: The wheels on the buggy go round all day long, so…

Bad Macho Wank!
The new BMW 3 Series Convertible

2000: Bad macho wank!

CARS = WEAPONS OF MASS
" KILLERS
DESTRUCTION
FIGHT BACK
OUSE REMOVALS

2014: Cars = weapons of mass destruction

Cars...

To admire top models with great curves
visit Carbase!
STILL NOT TRAVELLING
VERY FAR THEN...
SAME OLD POLLUTING
TRANSPORT AND SEXIST ADVERTISING!
CARBASE

2017: Still not travelling very far then… same old polluting transport and sexist advertising

ELECTIONS 2005 AND 2010...

More original and subvertised billboards from 7 General Elections (1992 – 2017) at www.flickr.com/photos/donpedro

BLAIR'S MUM
BLAIR'S BROTHER
A BLAIR CLONE
Longest period of economic growth for 200 years with Labour. Let's take Britain forward not back.
Labour
JCDecaux
4.1m
13'-6"
No 1
UNIT
BMF

"I was only seven
but I'll never forget
repossession."
GOVERNMENT=POVERTY
CLEARCHANNEL

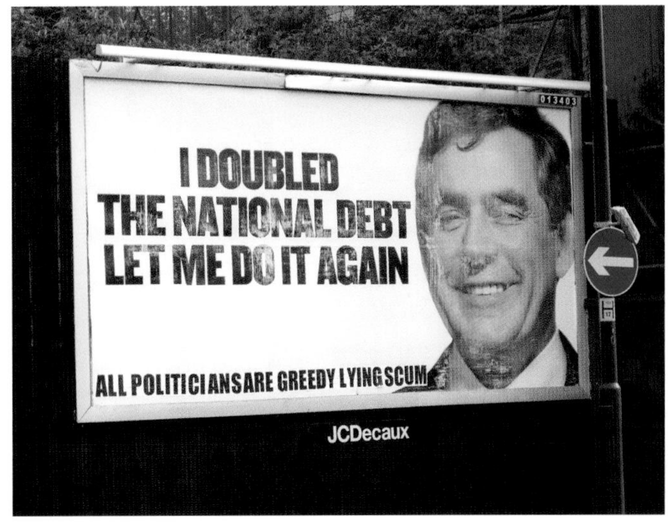
I DOUBLED
THE NATIONAL DEBT
LET ME DO IT AGAIN
ALL POLITICIANSARE GREEDY LYINGSCUM
JCDecaux

LET'S HAVE NATIONAL
CITIZEN SERVICE
FOR 16 YEAR-OLDS
DONT
Vote Conservativ

It's not racist
to impose limits
on immigration.
AND PIGS CAN FLY
YOU THINKING WHAT WE'RE THINKING? NO!
CONSERVATIVE

Above - 2005: Government = poverty | 2010: All politicians are greedy lying scum | 2005: It's not racist to impose limits on immigration | 2010: Don't vote Conservative |

Left - 2005: Blair's mum, Blair's brother, a Blair clone [senior Conservatives Margaret Thatcher, John Major, Michael Howard]

AUSTERITY AND CUTS...

SOCIAL MOBILITY: OUR LOWEST EVER!
BANK BAILOUT: NO MONEY BACK GUARANTEE!
(UNIVERSITY) EDUCATION: YOURS FOR ONLY £50K!
LAST-SEASON ITEMS!: SOCIAL HOUSING
OSBORNE'S XMAS SALE!
TOP TAX-RATE, CORPORATION TAX UNBEATABLE DISCOUNTS!!
TAX-AVOIDERS: MASSIVE SAVINGS!
Austerity: Pay Now. Pay Later!
KNOCK-DOWN LIVING STANDARDS!
EVERYTHING MUST GO!
PUBLIC SERVICES, WELFARE, JOBS...
2-4-1 SCAPEGOATING & RACISM!
10% EXTRA: MPS SALARIES!
NHS GIVEAWAY!!
50% OFF!! COUNCIL BUDGETS
REDUCED!!! HEALTH & SOCIAL CARE, PENSIONS, WAGES
COMPARE NOW
12 ALTERNATIVES TO AUSTERITY AND THE CUTS!
Public Ownership of Public Services - reverse privatisation of Railways, Energy and the NHS!
A Living Wage For All, abolish Zero-hour contracts & end the wage freeze!
Fairer taxes... Restore 50p Top Tax-rate/28% Corporation Tax & Reform Council Tax so wealthier pay more!
Clamp Down on Tax Avoidance/Evasion - reclaim the £billions owed to the public!
Banking for People not Profits: a publicly-owned, democratic banking system!
New taxes on the rich: 'Robin Hood' Financial Tax & Empty Property Tax to tackle inequality & the housing crisis.
Invest in building Social Housing, scrap the Bedroom Tax & cap private rents!
A Green DEAL - 1 million climate jobs, insulate our homes & stable renewable energy supply!
More power to local people: give Councils more control over budgets and reverse the cuts!
End the cost of war in blood & money... No military interventions. No Trident replacement.
Free University/vocational Education & quality Apprenticeships for young people: proper funding!
Save on Private Consultants to the state (£2.8bn), charging fat-cat fees for little obvious benefit!
BRISTOL PEOPLE'S ASSEMBLY #AUSTERITYFAIL @BRISTOLPA GET INVOLVED!
BRISTOLPEOPLESASSEMBLY@GMAIL.COM BRISTOLPEOPLESASSEMBLY.ORG
FACEBOOK.COM/BRISTOLPEOPLESASSEMBLY

2015: Osborne's xmas sale [www.facebook.com/peoplesassembly]

MAKING CUTS
IN A RECESSION
IS NOT ONLY
BAD ECONOMICS
IT IS SHEER
STUPIDITY!!!

2010: Making cuts in a recession [This gentleman also made the point that the lower socio-economic classes (C, D, E) were paying for the mistakes of classes A and B]

STOP THE CU*TS!
10
Demonstration Saturday October 23rd
11.00am from

EASTON SAYS
NO CUTS!

FEEL WARM INSIDE
BURN THE CON-DEMS!
PRICE FREEZE
GUARANTEE
eDF
ENERGY
primesight

since 2010, there has
been a 300% increase
in food bank usage

Clockwise from top left - 2010: Stop the cu*ts! | 2011: Easton says no cuts! Facebook 'Easton against the cuts' [www.bristoanticutsalliance.org.uk] | 2013: Since 2010 there has been a 300% increase in food bank usage | 2010: Feel warm inside - Burn the Con-Dems! |

Make them learn English
Cut English classes
MONDAYS 1
WE WOR
YOU MA
The
Shi
14 R

NO MORE AUSTERITY
NO CUTS
DEMAND THE ALTERNATIVE: SAT 21 JUNE
NATIONAL DEMONSTRATION + FREE FESTIVAL
ASSEMBLE: 1PM, BBC HQ, PORTLAND PLACE
LONDON W1 1AA (NEAREST TUBE: OXFORD CIRCUS)
THEPEOPLESASSEMBLY.ORG.UK
THE PEOPLE'S ASSEMBLY

BRISTOL CITY COUNCIL
AXE THE BEDROOM TAX

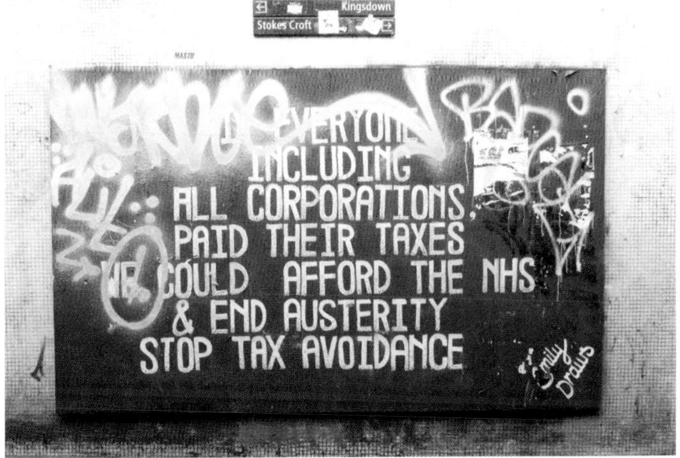
Kingsdown
Stokes Croft
EVERYONE INCLUDING ALL CORPORATIONS PAID THEIR TAXES WE COULD AFFORD THE NHS & END AUSTERITY
STOP TAX AVOIDANCE
Emily Draws

Clockwise from top left - 2011: Make them learn English. Cut English lessons | 2014: No more austerity | 2015: If everyone including all corporations paid their taxes | 2013: Axe the bedroom tax|

POLICE...

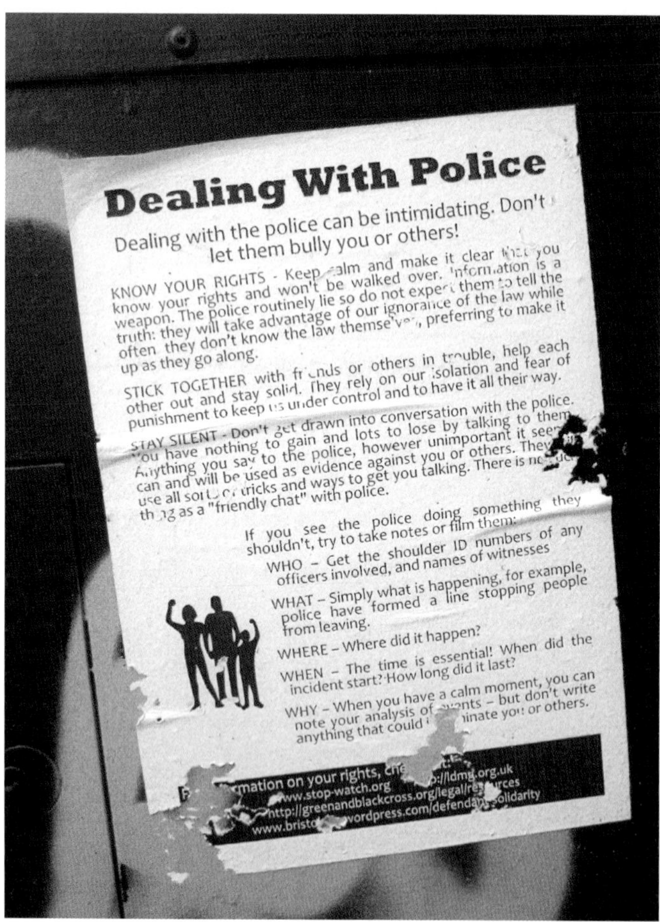
Dealing With Police
Dealing with the police can be intimidating. Don't let them bully you or others!
KNOW YOUR RIGHTS - Keep alm and make it clear you know your rights and won't be walked over. is a weapon. The police routinely lie so do not expe them to tell the truth: they will take advantage of our ignorance of the law while often they don't know the law , preferring to make it up as they go along.
STICK TOGETHER with or others in trouble, help each other out and stay They rely on our solation and fear of punishment to keep under control and to have it all their way.
STAY SILENT - Don't drawn into conversation with the police. ou have nothing to gain and lots to lose by talking to them nything you say to the police, however unimportant it see can and will be used as evidence against you or others. They use all tricks and ways to get you talking. There is as a "friendly chat" with police.
If you see the police doing something they shouldn't, try to take notes or film them:
WHO – Get the shoulder ID numbers of any officers involved, and names of witnesses
WHAT – Simply what is happening, for example, police have formed a line stopping people from leaving.
WHERE – Where did it happen?
WHEN – The time is essential! When did the incident start? How long did it last?
WHY – When you have a calm moment, you can note your analysis of – but don't write anything that could inate you or others.
mation on your rights,
www.stop-watch.org
ldmg.org.uk
greenandblackcross.org/legal/re
wordpress.com/defend olidarity

2014: Dealing with police [www.stop-watch.org]

Since 1990,
1510 people
have died in police
custody or following
police contact.
Not a single officer
has been convicted
for any of their deaths.
Getting away with it since 1829
#ACAB
METROPOLITAN POLICE
TOTAL MURDERERS

2017: Getting away with it since 1829

Disband the Met's Domestic Extremism Unit
'Domestic Extremist' means whatever the police want it to mean.

#WeDoNotConsent
RECKLESS LAW-BREAKING DEPRESSING VIOLENT
HUMILIATING RACIST MURDERERS
THUGS LIARS ARROGANT CORRUPT
DIVISIVE DANGEROUS
SLIMEY DECEPTIVE OPAQUE JUMPED-UP
OPPRESSIVE PROFILING POWER
INSTRUMENTS OF THE STATE FACIST TRIPPING
TERRIFYING BARBARIC PRICKS
INTIMIDATING BULLYING SMUG
ABUSIVE PETTY MORONIC
LONDONS BIGGEST GANG ABOMINABLE
TOTAL CUNTS
www.strikemag.org

THIS IS WHAT POLICE COMMUNITY RACE RELATIONS LOOKS LIKE.
STOP POLICE HARASSMENT, BRUTALITY AND RACISM!

ANARCHIST FEDERATION
AF
AFED.ORG.UK
If cats could talk to cops they wouldn't

Clockwise from top left - 2017: Disband the Met's Domestic Extremism Unit | 2014: Total cunts [www.strikemag.org] | 2016: If cats could talk to cops they wouldn't [afed.org.uk] | 2017: This is what police community race relations looks like |

BRISTOL ISSUES...

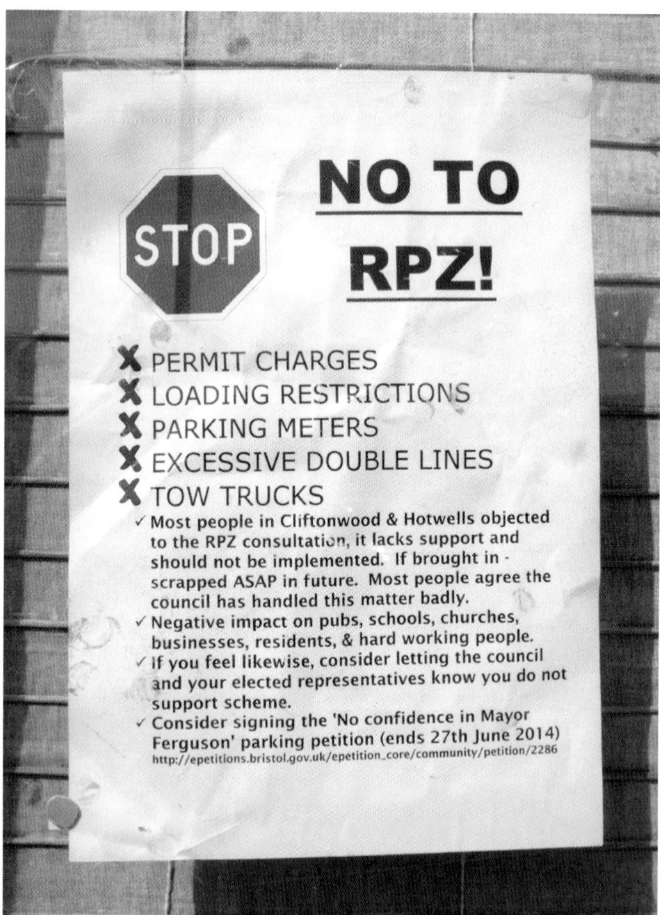
STOP
NO TO
RPZ!
PERMIT CHARGES
LOADING RESTRICTIONS
PARKING METERS
EXCESSIVE DOUBLE LINES
TOW TRUCKS
Most people in Cliftonwood & Hotwells objected to the RPZ consultation, it lacks support and should not be implemented. If brought in - scrapped ASAP in future. Most people agree the council has handled this matter badly.
Negative impact on pubs, schools, churches, businesses, residents, & hard working people.
If you feel likewise, consider letting the council and your elected representatives know you do not support scheme.
Consider signing the 'No confidence in Mayor Ferguson' parking petition (ends 27th June 2014)
http://epetitions.bristol.gov.uk/epetition_core/community/petition/2286

2014: No to RPZ! [resident parking zones]

HIRE
£50, capacity of 35 people
info@theartshouse.org or text 07805 62379
LOVE STOKES CROFT,
SAVE HAMILTON HOUSE!
#SAVEHAMILTONHOUSE
Here

2017: Love Stokes Croft Save Hamilton House [The property company that owns the building are threatening some or all tenants (charities, social enterprises, artists, therapists, etc) with eviction]

Vote for
Real Change
Green Party
Bedroom Tax evictions
Buy yourself a Council House
(in defiance of party policy)
Put up Council Tax
Put up Council Tenants' rent
Ship Bristol's waste to Sweden
(to be burnt in an incinerator)
Poisonous for ALL
In BRISTOL WEST
Greedy GUS

2015: Vote for Real Change [Gus Hoyt, Green Party councillor]

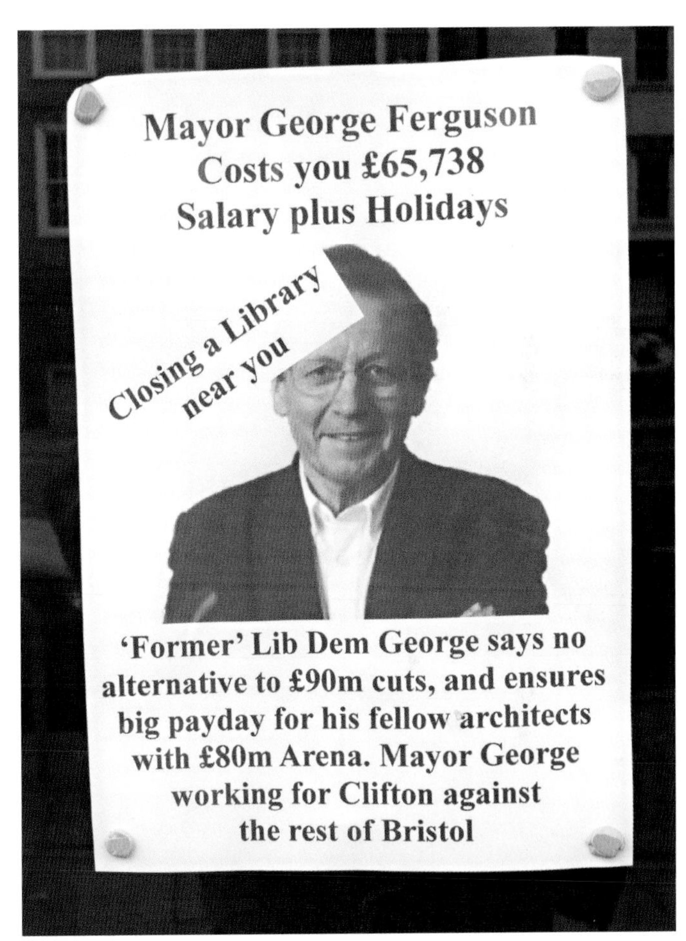
Mayor George Ferguson
Costs you £65,738
Salary plus Holidays
Closing a Library
near you
'Former' Lib Dem George says no alternative to £90m cuts, and ensures big payday for his fellow architects with £80m Arena. Mayor George working for Clifton against the rest of Bristol

2013: Mayor George Ferguson costs you

George Ferguson was the red trouser wearing independent Mayor of Bristol from 2012 to 2016. His constant presence in mainstream and social media made him very well known. His attempts to address congestion and parking issues were especially controversial.

It doesn't stop here
2016
RED TROUSERED GREENWASH
BRISTOL 2015
JCDecaux

GENTRIFERGUSON
OBEY
OBEY
OBEY

THE DICTATOR
OBEY
THE DICTATOR

CLEARCHANNEL
THE THICK ONE.
i'm lovin' it
20
ENJOY
GEORGE FERGUSON
CLEARCHANNEL

Clockwise from top left - 2016: Red trousered greenwash [The running of Bristol's European Green Capital 2015 programme drew criticism, some of which was aimed at the Mayor] | 2014: Gentriferguson | 2013: The thick one | 2013: The Dictator/Obey |

WINDSCREENS
TO LET
FEED THE CHILDREN
TAXI
NO TEMPLE MEADS TAXI PERMITS

BUS RAPID TRANSIT 2
RESIDENTS SAY
NO buses over Ashton Ave bridge
We say Hotwell Road option or bin BRT2

Say No To McDonald's in Fishponds! #NoMacInF
BURGER OFF!
#NoMacInF
SAY NO TO MCDONALD'S DRIVE THRU IN FISHPONDS
PROTEST
25th March 10.30 @ Old Bristol Tile Site
OBJECT
Meet @ City Hall 20th April 9am
Say No to McDonald's in Fishponds
#NoMacInF @NoMcInFishponds
POLLUTION NOISE
Say No To McDonald's in Fishponds! #NoMacInF

CRAP.
BRISTOL CITY COUNCIL
EASTON RENEWAL AREA

Clockwise from top left - 2012: No Temple Meads taxi permits | 2013: No buses over Ashton Ave bridge [stopbrt2.org.uk]| 2017: Crap | 2017: Burger off! |

AND THE REST...

For the photos that don't fit neatly into a category.

SMOKERS
PLEASE
DO NOT
OBSTRUCT
THIS
FOOTPATH
ITS YOUR FREEDOM TO CHOOSE
ANTI-SMOKING LEGISLATION, DID YOU GET ASKED?
DID THEY GIVE YOU A CHOICE?
YOUR PARENTS & GRAND PARENTS FOUGHT IN TWO WORLD WARS FOR YOUR FREEDOM, YOUR FREEDOM TO CHOOSE, TO HAVE YOUR SAY
ITS TIME TO REMIND THE GOVERNMENT WHO VOTED FOR THEM
YOU ARE TOLD DON'T LEAVE YOUR DRINKS UNATTENDED, YOU ARE TOLD DON'T DRINK OUTSIDE YOUR LOCAL
IT'S TIME TO TELL THEM NO
WE WANT THE RIGHT TO CHOOSE
GIVE YOUR SUPPORT, CONTACT:
EDDIE ROGERS - eddierogers@tiscali.co.uk - 01736 369918 or 07980816801
VIV EVANS - 07824619260 vivscuk@aol.com
Please Sign Sheet Behind Bar
ITS YOUR FREEDOM TO CHOOSE
ANTI-SMOKING LEGISLATION, DID YOU GET ASKED?
DID THEY GIVE YOU A CHOICE?
NO, INSTEAD THEY MADE YOU FEEL LIKE AN OUTCAST IN SOCIETY
THEY COULD MAKE PUBS & CLUBS SMOKING & NON SMOKING, THEN YOU COULD DECIDE
NO, BUT THEY ARE HAPPY TO COLLECT THE TAXES?
ITS TIME TO REMIND THE GOVERNMENT WHO THE VOTERS ARE
GIVE YOUR SUPPORT, CONTACT:
EDDIE ROGERS - eddierogers@tiscali.co.uk 01736 369918 or 07980816801
VIV EVANS - 07824619260 vivscuk@aol.com
IF YOU DON'T SAY NO, WHO WILL ?

2007: Its your freedom to choose [The smoking ban in public places in England came into force on 1 July 2007]

SCRAP THE KETTLE!

FUCK OFF
FASCISTS
RACISTS
ANTISEMITES
SPECIESISTS
SEXISTS
HOMOPHOBISTS
NATIONALISTS
PATRIOTS!

THE ROYAL INTERNATIONAL
AIR TATTOO
BAE SYSTEMS
RAF Fairford
Near Swindon
16-17 July 2011
REMEMBER
BRIAN HAW
JCDecaux

SAY NO
·WAR
·LAW
·HATE
·PLASTIC
·WORK
·CARS
SAY YES
·PEACE
·FREEDOM
·LOVE
·HEMP
·PLAY
·BIKES

NO GOD
NO STATE
NO LIES

CYCLIST
DISMOUNT

ERACISM

APATHY = COLLABORATION

casualisation
kills
www.simonjones.org.uk

Top row from left - 2009: Scrap the kettle [The kettle is a policing method used during demonstrations] | 2012: Fuck off | 2011: Remember Brian Haw [Peace campaigner who set up a camp in London's Parliament Square in 2001 in protest against UK and US foreign policy. He died in 2011] | Middle row - 2007: Say no say yes | 2010: No God no state no lies | 2016: No bikes!!! | Bottom row - 2007: Eracism | 2002: Apathy = collaboration | 2010: Casualisation kills [www.simonjones.org.uk]

2008: The Oil Apocalypse - Coming to a Civilization near you...

[Our economies and way of life are extremely dependent on oil. However, as a finite resource, sooner or later supplies will dwindle, with more far-reaching consequences than most of us can imagine. Everything will change. Look up 'peak oil', or see the film 'A Crude Awakening' to find out more]

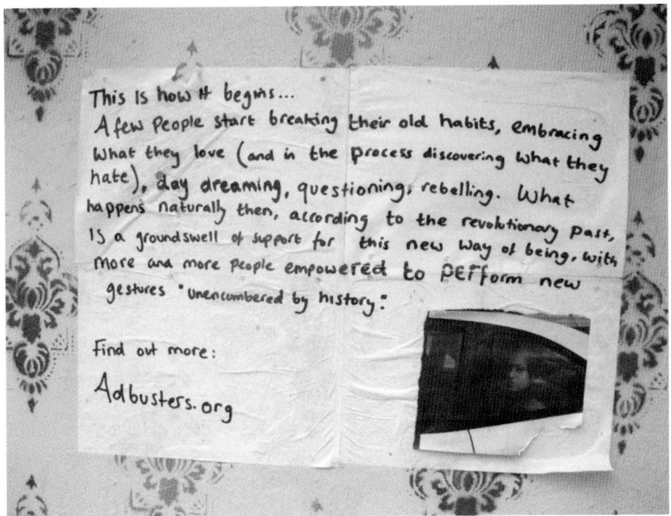
This is how it begins...
A few people start breaking their old habits, embracing what they love (and in the process discovering what they hate), day dreaming, questioning, rebelling. What happens naturally then, according to the revolutionary past, is a groundswell of support for this new way of being, with more and more people empowered to perform new gestures "unencumbered by history."
Find out more:
Adbusters.org

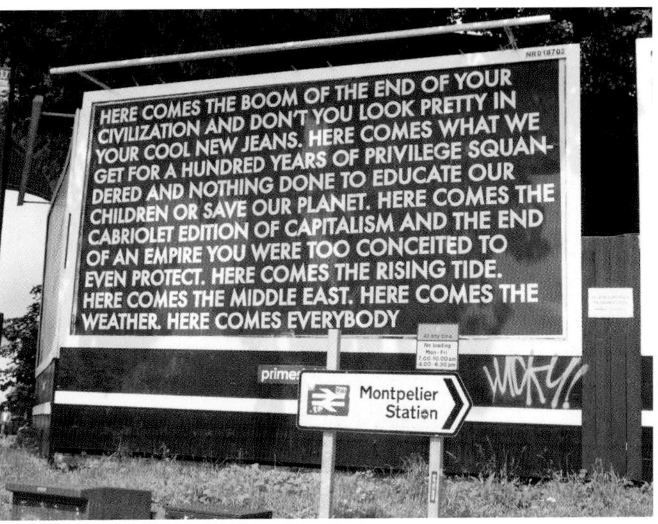
HERE COMES THE BOOM OF THE END OF YOUR CIVILIZATION AND DON'T YOU LOOK PRETTY IN YOUR COOL NEW JEANS. HERE COMES WHAT WE GET FOR A HUNDRED YEARS OF PRIVILEGE SQUANDERED AND NOTHING DONE TO EDUCATE OUR CHILDREN OR SAVE OUR PLANET. HERE COMES THE CABRIOLET EDITION OF CAPITALISM AND THE END OF AN EMPIRE YOU WERE TOO CONCEITED TO EVEN PROTECT. HERE COMES THE RISING TIDE. HERE COMES THE MIDDLE EAST. HERE COMES THE WEATHER. HERE COMES EVERYBODY
Montpelier Station

LEGAL NAME FRAUD
THE TRUTH
IT'S ILLEGAL TO USE A LEGAL NAME
ASK PC MARK KENNEDY
primesight

THERE'S ONLY ONE
HUTTON'S WHITE WASH
YELLOW PAGES
MAIDEN-HARLECH

Clockwise from top left – 2010: This is how it begins [adbusters.org] | 2012: Here comes the boom | 2004: There's only one Hutton's whitewash [the Hutton Inquiry on with the death of David Kelly, a former UN weapons inspector named as the source of quotes made by the BBC – to the effect that the Labour government sexed up its report into Iraq and weapons of mass destruction, a critical factor in Parliamentary and public support for going to war with Iraq. Several national newspapers accused the enquiry of "an establishment whitewash"] | 2014: Ask PC Mark Kennedy [This undercover Metropolitan Police officer in the domestic extremists unit infiltrated environmental and other groups, and had long-term intimate relationships with activists]

THATCHER is DEAD!
She should go down in history...
...as a warmonger
destroyer of
communities,
and divider of society.
Who sold off
our housing,
railways and
energy system
...and left us at the
mercy of the bankers!
May she burn in hell!

2013: Thatcher is dead!

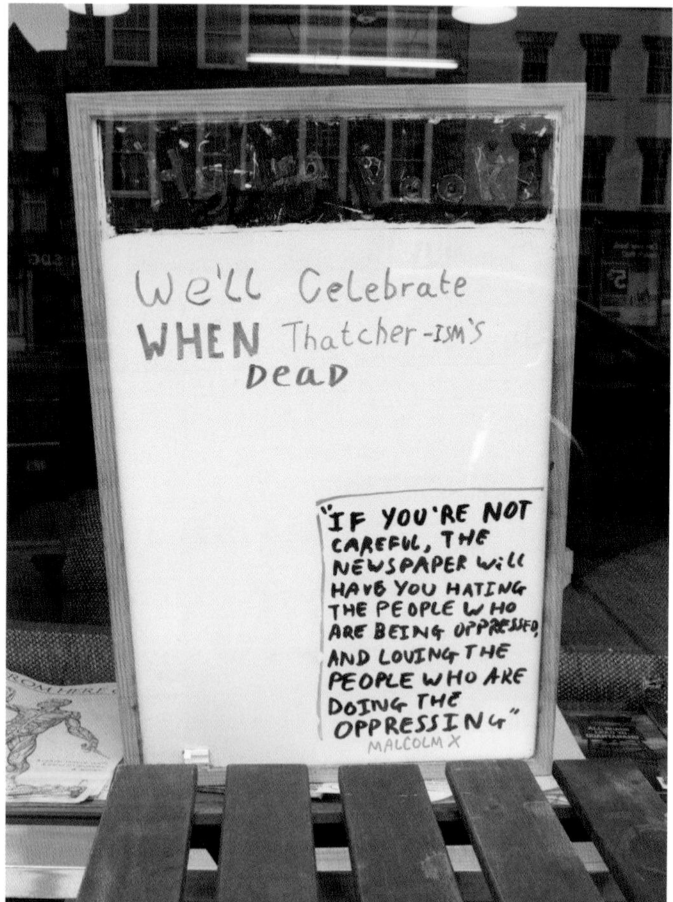
We'll Celebrate
WHEN Thatcher-ISM'S
DEAD
"IF YOU'RE NOT CAREFUL, THE NEWSPAPER WILL HAVE YOU HATING THE PEOPLE WHO ARE BEING OPPRESSED, AND LOVING THE PEOPLE WHO ARE DOING THE OPPRESSING"
MALCOLM X

2013: We'll celebrate when Thatcherism's dead

[Margaret Thatcher was so despised by some, that there was a long-standing arrangement for a party to take place on Trafalgar Square at 6pm on the Saturday after her death]

And the rest...

Britain's biggest break
12 MAR 04
There's no better break than a KitKat break
Britain's Biggest Break 12/3/04 3pm
KitKat
INVESTMENT QUESTIONS?
WE HAVE LOTS OF ANSWERS.
OK - WHERE'S MY
FUCKING PENSION GONE?
NORWICH UNION

WE WANT A DECENT PENSION.
STOP SPENDING CUTS.
STOP BOMBING LIBYA.
USE THIS MONEY TO IMPROVE
OUR HOSPITALS AND
CARE FOR THE ELDERLY.

SAVE STATE
PENSIONS

RAMP-AGE
PENSIONER POWER

From top left. 2004: OK - Where's my fucking pension gone? {Pension funds are vulnerable if companies decide to use them to shore up their business, or if investments collapse. The Mirror Group under Robert Maxwell famously stole their employee's company pensions in 1999] | 2011: We want a decent pension stop spending ours | 2011: Ramp-age - Pensioner power | 2005: Save state pensions |

BRITAIN
OUT
OF EUROPE!

2001: Britain out of Europe

And the rest...

£ SAVE THE POUND £
EUROS NOT WELCOME

2002: Save the pound, Euros not welcome

BRISTOL
Straight Talking Property
FOR A SUSTAINABLE
FUTURE
Go and make disciples
of all nations
and say no to war
and illegal drugs
Life would be better
There is no harm in it
THINK ABOUT IT!

2014: Straight talking property

LOVE
FASHION
HATE
SWEATSHOPS
waronwant.org/lovefashionhatesweatshops

2016: Love fashion hate sweatshops [waronwant.org/lovefashionhatesweatshops]

And the rest...

FREE CHELSEA MANNING
privatemanning.org
Heroic WikiLeaks whistle-blower
Blowing the whistle on war crimes is not a crime

2016: Free Chelsea Manning [Leaked US military documents, including videos of air strikes in Iraq. Her 35 year sentence was overruled by President Obama and she was released in 2017 after serving 4 years. privatemanning.org]

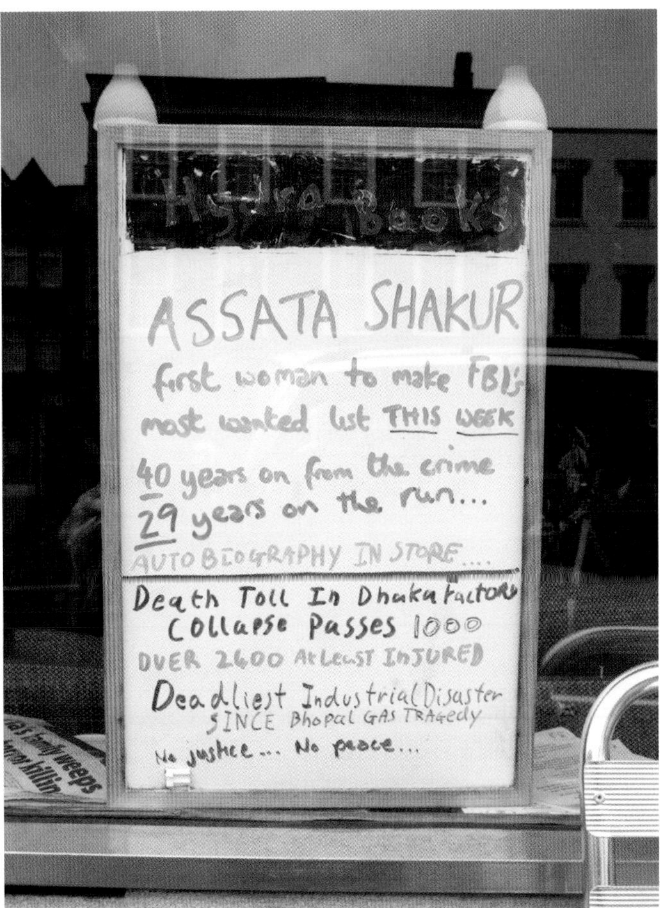
Hydra Books
ASSATA SHAKUR
first woman to make FBI's most wanted list THIS WEEK
40 years on from the crime
29 years on the run...
AUTOBIOGRAPHY IN STORE...
Death Toll In Dhaka Factory Collapse Passes 1000
OVER 2600 At Least INJURED
Deadliest Industrial Disaster SINCE Bhopal GAS TRAGEDY
No justice... No peace...

2013: Assata Shakur [former member of the Black Liberation Army, a black nationalist urban guerrilla group. Convicted in 1977 of the first-degree murder of a State Trooper during a shootout in 1973. She escaped from prison in 1979 and fled to Cuba, where she was granted political asylum]. Death toll in Dhaka factory collapse passes 1000

Building an Anarchist Future

Every year seems to bring more bad news; the poor have to pay for the mistakes of the rich. The cuts, as predicted, have hit the poorest hardest, hammering education, benefits, pensions, housing and the NHS.

At the same time, global climate change and corporate land exploitation have caused extreme weather patterns, pushing entire ecosystems closer to the brink. The arms trade, wars for oil, and extreme right-wing politics stir up conflict across the Middle East and beyond, pushing ordinary people into desperate life-threatening situations.

However, there is hope, and people have been fighting back, through strikes, direct action and the taking up of arms. Capitalism isn't working, and reformism has failed. People want change. But if capitalism collapsed tomorrow, we ask ourselves:

Would we be ready?

As anarchists, we spend a lot of time fighting against oppressive structures, but we also discuss our hopes and dreams for a new, more equal world – that of anarchism. We have developed concepts around mutual aid, solidarity, co-operation, direct action, equality, and non-hierarchical organisation, but how do we put these into practice?

At this year's Bristol Anarchist Bookfair, we want to create a space for people to explore these ideas, whether you are new to the concept or an old hand. How will we create a better, more equal society, so that people will feel safe and accepted whatever their sexual orientation, gender, ability, race or age? How will we hold people to account for their actions if we abolish prisons and the police? If revolutions happen tomorrow, we won't have all the answers, and an anarchist society will not occur overnight – there will be ongoing change and adaptation. But the core principles of anarchism offer us the building blocks for the future, and a roadmap on how to get there.

Let's be ready!

Stalls • Workshops
Radical History Zone
Wheelchair Accessible
Art Space
Vegan Cafe
Kids' Space
Free Entry
tol
kfair
st Future
ir.org

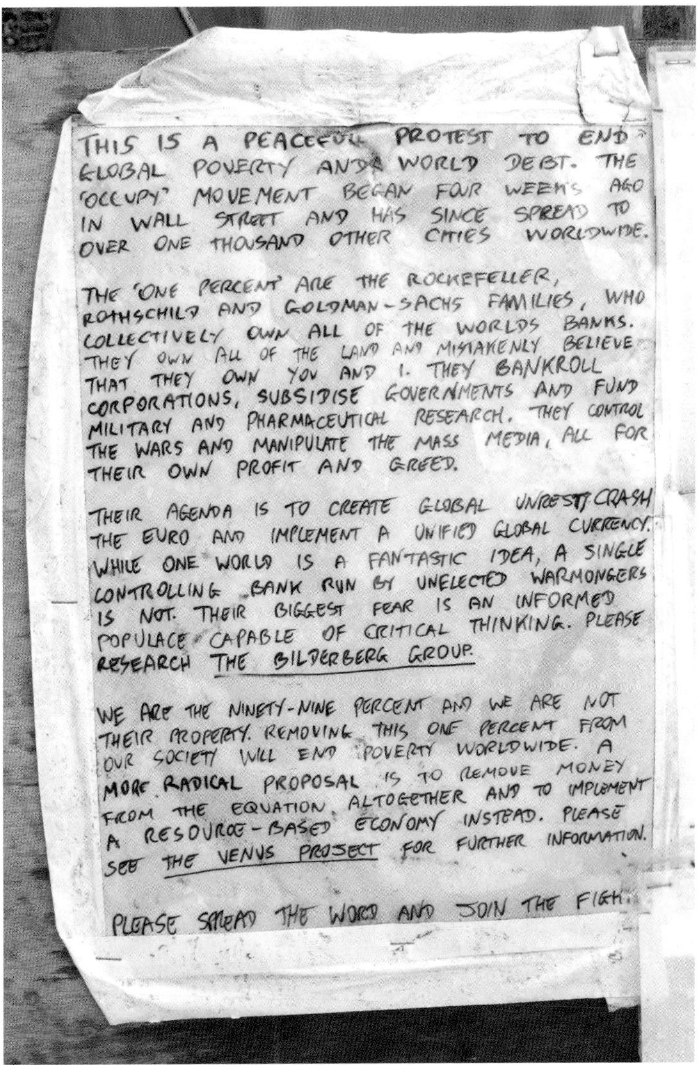
THIS IS A PEACEFUL PROTEST TO END GLOBAL POVERTY AND WORLD DEBT. THE 'OCCUPY' MOVEMENT BEGAN FOUR WEEKS AGO IN WALL STREET AND HAS SINCE SPREAD TO OVER ONE THOUSAND OTHER CITIES WORLDWIDE.
THE 'ONE PERCENT' ARE THE ROCKEFELLER, ROTHSCHILD AND GOLDMAN-SACHS FAMILIES, WHO COLLECTIVELY OWN ALL OF THE WORLDS BANKS. THEY OWN ALL OF THE LAND AND MISTAKENLY BELIEVE THAT THEY OWN YOU AND I. THEY BANKROLL CORPORATIONS, SUBSIDISE GOVERNMENTS AND FUND MILITARY AND PHARMACEUTICAL RESEARCH. THEY CONTROL THE WARS AND MANIPULATE THE MASS MEDIA, ALL FOR THEIR OWN PROFIT AND GREED.
THEIR AGENDA IS TO CREATE GLOBAL UNREST, CRASH THE EURO AND IMPLEMENT A UNIFIED GLOBAL CURRENCY. WHILE ONE WORLD IS A FANTASTIC IDEA, A SINGLE CONTROLLING BANK RUN BY UNELECTED WARMONGERS IS NOT. THEIR BIGGEST FEAR IS AN INFORMED POPULACE CAPABLE OF CRITICAL THINKING. PLEASE RESEARCH THE BILDERBERG GROUP.
WE ARE THE NINETY-NINE PERCENT AND WE ARE NOT THEIR PROPERTY. REMOVING THIS ONE PERCENT FROM OUR SOCIETY WILL END POVERTY WORLDWIDE. A MORE RADICAL PROPOSAL IS TO REMOVE MONEY FROM THE EQUATION ALTOGETHER AND TO IMPLEMENT A RESOURCE-BASED ECONOMY INSTEAD. PLEASE SEE THE VENUS PROJECT FOR FURTHER INFORMATION.
PLEASE SPREAD THE WORD AND JOIN THE FIGHT

Above - 2011: This is a peaceful protest
[Location: Occupy Nottingham]

Left – 2016: Building an anarchist future

PROTECT
OUR KERB
APPEAL

DRIVE
IN
ROAD

DON'T DRIVE
OVER
HISTORY

RESPECT
TYRED
KERBS

KEEP
WHEELS
ON ROAD

DRIVING
TEST

KERB
ANTISOCIAL
BEHAVIOUR

KEEP
OFF
PAVEMENT

2016: Kerb protest

And the rest...

This Land Is Your Land
Words and Music by Woody Guthrie
This land is your lånd this land is my land
From California to the New York island;
From the red wood forest to the Gulf Stream waters
This land was made for you and me.
As I was walking that ribbon of highway,
I saw above me that endless skyway:
I saw below me that golden valley:
This land was made for you and me.
I've roamed and rambled and I followed my footsteps
To the sparkling sands of her diamond deserts;
And all around me a voice was sounding:
This land was made for you and me.
When the sun came shining, and I was strolling,
And the wheat fields waving and the dust clouds rolling,
As the fog was lifting a voice was chanting:
This land was made for you and me.
As I went walking I saw a sign there
And on the sign it said "No Trespassing."
But on the other side it didn't say nothing,
That side was made for you and me.
In the shadow of the steeple I saw my people,
By the relief office I seen my people;
As they stood there hungry, I stood there asking
Is this land made for you and me?
Nobody living can ever stop me,
As I go walking that freedom highway;
Nobody living can ever make me turn back
This land was made for you and me.

2013: St Werburgh's allotment protest [against the threatened sale of the land for development. Bristol City Council bought the land, the allotments were saved. The song lyrics on the fence are Woody Guthrie's 'This Land Is Your land']

THE GOD
THE GOD BOX IS THIS MAGIC DEVICE, INVADE OUR LIVES
OUR BRAINS ARE SLICED - MADE FOR CONFUSION, INTRUSION
& FABRICATION - NEWS & BLUES TO CHANGE THE NATION
WAR & PRODUCTS NOT INFORMATION. ALL THIS SHIT
PUMPED INTO OUR HEARTS & SOUL COS TESCO &
NATWEST WANT YOUR DOUGH - WATCH IF YOU WANT
BUT ITS STUNTS YOUR GROWTH. MANIPULATES RIGHT
TO THE CORE, COS ITS THE LATEST LIPPY & NOKIAS OUR
CHILDREN SAW — YOU KNOW WHAT... RICH OR POOR,
SMASH THAT DOOR & LETS CONNECT, COS ALL
WE DO IS DISCONNECT & DO U KNOW THE FULL EFFECT?
WE MAY AS WELL GET SOME K & SMACK & HIT THE DECK
BUT ITS ALREADY HAPPEND LETS INTERCEPT, FUCK TV
LETS INTERGECT. THERES LIFE OUTSIDE WHILE WE ALL SLEPT
F>11...... (YES I KNOW I CANT SPELL)
DAEWOO
FUCK OFF HOME &
WATCH THE

2011: The God Box [in a Temporary Autononomous Art exhibition]

And the rest...

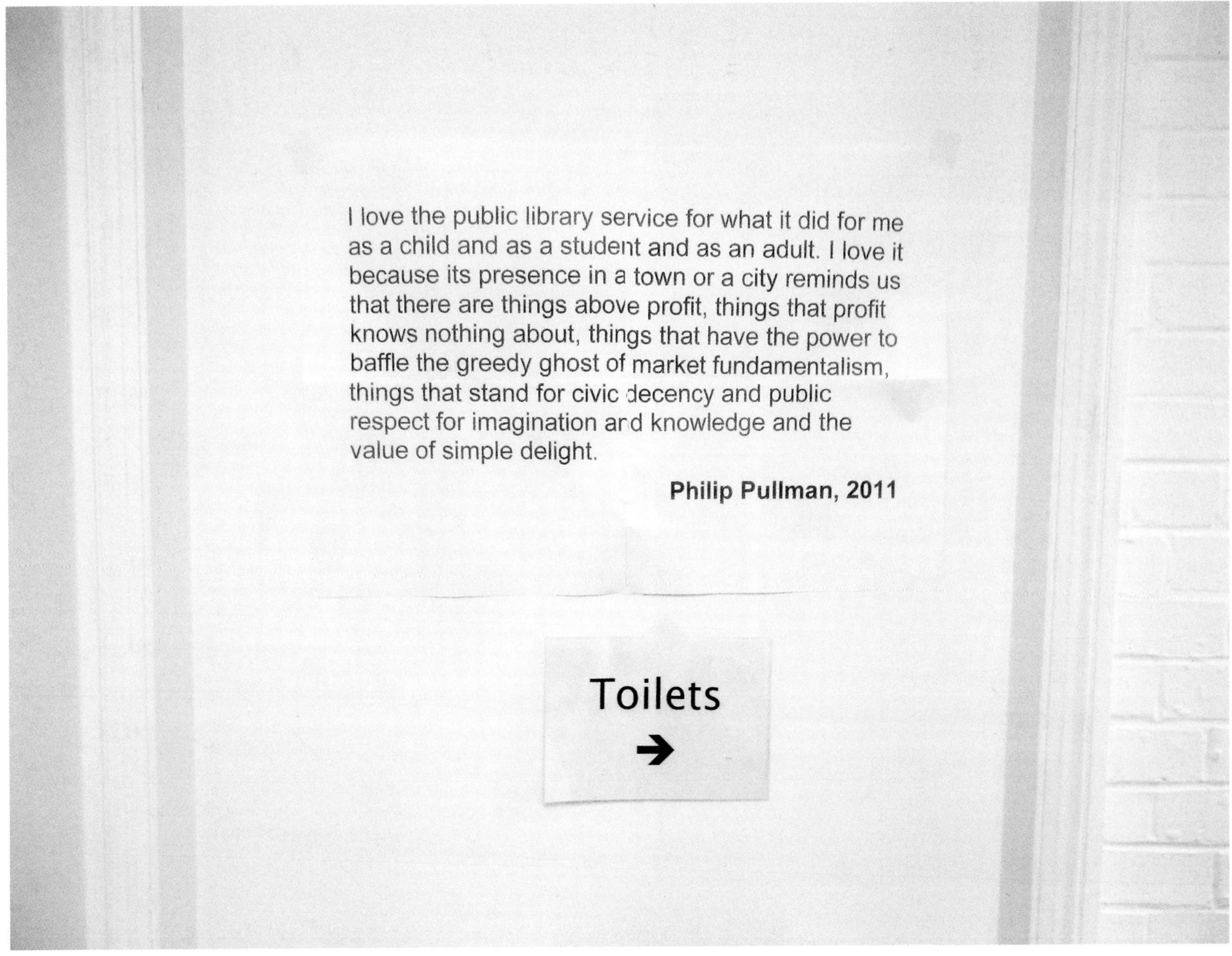
I love the public library service for what it did for me as a child and as a student and as an adult. I love it because its presence in a town or a city reminds us that there are things above profit, things that profit knows nothing about, things that have the power to baffle the greedy ghost of market fundamentalism, things that stand for civic decency and public respect for imagination and knowledge and the value of simple delight.
Philip Pullman, 2011
Toilets
➔

2011: I love the public library service...
[Author Philip Pullman defending libraries against local government expenditure cuts]

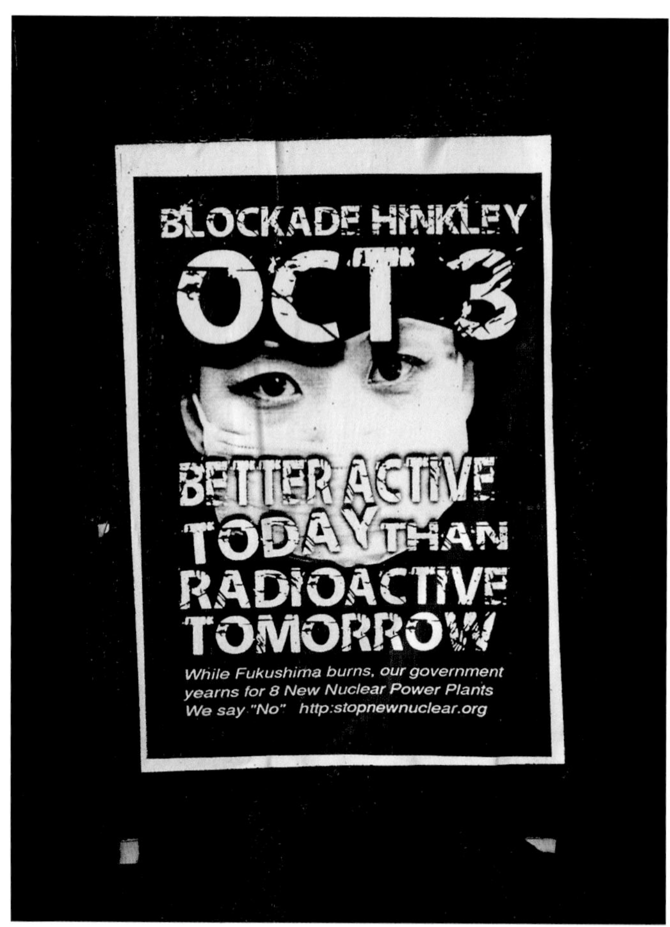
BLOCKADE HINKLEY
OCT 3
BETTER ACTIVE
TODAY THAN
RADIOACTIVE
TOMORROW
While Fukushima burns, our government
yearns for 8 New Nuclear Power Plants
We say "No" http:stopnewnuclear.org

NOT CLEAN
NOT SAFE
NOT CLEVER
"No Generation should
impose on future generations
those problems to which it
has no solutions"
Jonathon Porrit
STOP HINKLEY C
www.stophinkley.org

2011: Blockade Hinkley [www.stopnewnuclear.org.uk]

2011: Not clean not safe not clever [www.stophinkley.org]

[The nuclear debate was given fresh impetus by the melt-downs, explosions and spent fuel fires at the Fukushima power complex in Japan in 2011, which created a major disaster for public health and the environment as well as Japan's economy. The UK government has given permission for private companies to build up to 8 new nuclear power stations, the first at Hinkley Point in Somerset]

BURN YOUR TV
BURN YOUR TV

DON'T BUY THE SUN
96
JUSTICE
FOR ALL
Hillsborough Justice Campaign

CLEARCHANNEL
"Sky+, it does your remembering for you"
THINKING
Sky+
sky
08442 41 42 43
CUSTOMER CAR PARK ONLY
CLAMPING IN PROGRESS
RELEASE FEE £50.00

250 BOX SETS.
MINDS
FORTITUDE
GREY'S ANATOMY
NOW TV
ENTERTAINMENT Pass
You. Sofa. Sorted.
DON'T WASTE YOUR LIFE WITH THIS !!!
primesight

Clockwise from top left - 2013: Burn your TV | 2014: Don't buy the Sun [Hillsborough football stadium disaster, 1989. Four days after the crush in which 96 people died and 766 were injured, an article in the Sun newspaper (headlined 'The Truth') made insensitive and untrue claims about the behaviour of Liverpool fans] | 2017: Don't waste your life with this | 2008: Sky, it does your thinking for you |

Stop the genocide
of Albino African's
Boycott the African
national Congress

AVENGE GRENFELL
CLASS WAR
RUSSELL TOWN AVE

ROSA
PARKS
LANE

bringbackbritishrail.org

911
WAS
AN
INSIDE
JOB

SURFERS AGAINST SEWAGE
SURFERS AGAINST SEWAGE
NO BUTTS ON THE BEACH
WWW.SAS.ORG.UK

INVEST YOUR TIME IN CREATING
A BETTER
FUTURE
PLSE
X

BEWARE!
Halal is barbaric and funds terrorism
#BanHalal

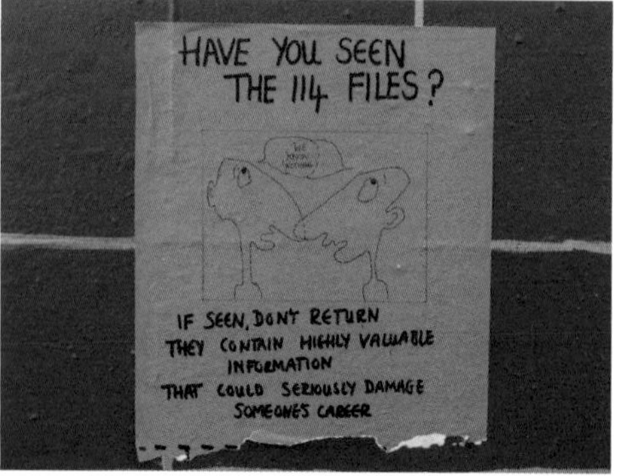
HAVE YOU SEEN
THE 114 FILES?
IF SEEN, DONT RETURN
THEY CONTAIN HIGHLY VALUABLE
INFORMATION
THAT COULD SERIOUSLY DAMAGE
SOMEONE'S CAREER

Top row from left - 2011: Stop the genocide of Albino African's | 2017: Avenge Grenfell, class war [fire at council block of flats, at least 87 people died] | 2017: Rosa Parks Lane [American civil rights activist who challenged segregation in 1955 and prompted the bus boycott led by Martin Luther King] | Middle row - 2012: bringbackbritishrail.org | 2011: 911 was an inside job | 2015: No butts on the beach [www.sas.org.uk] | Bottom row - 2017: Invest your time | 2016: Beware! Halal is barbaric and funds terrorism | 2016: Have you seen the 114 files? [The Home Office admitted that 114 files relating to allegations about historical sex abuse involving politicians are missing] |

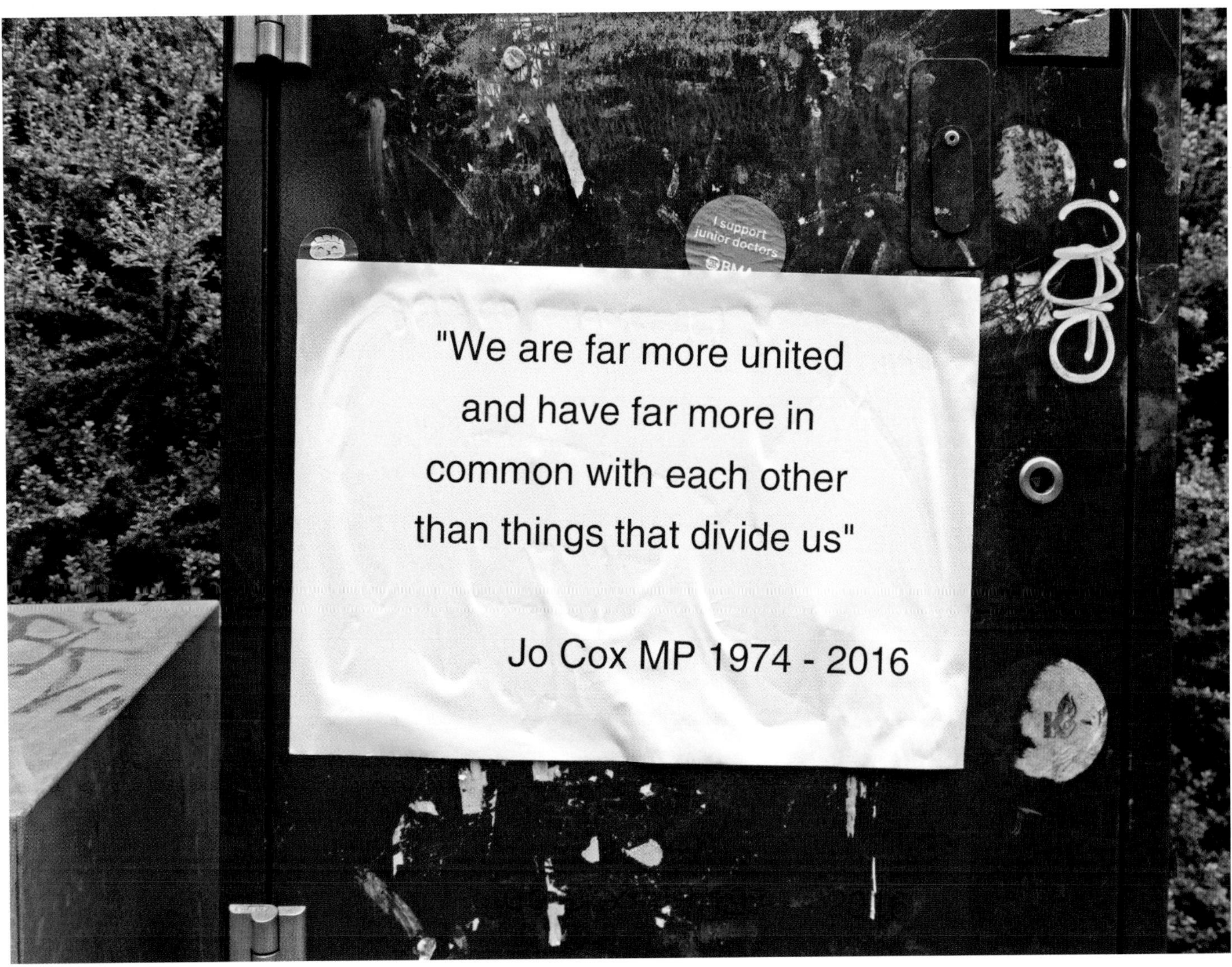
I support junior doctors
BMA
"We are far more united
and have far more in
common with each other
than things that divide us"
Jo Cox MP 1974 - 2016

2016: We are far more united [Labour MP Jo Cox was murdered by a man with a history of psychiatric problems and links to the US-based neo-Nazi group National Alliance. Source: Wikipedia]

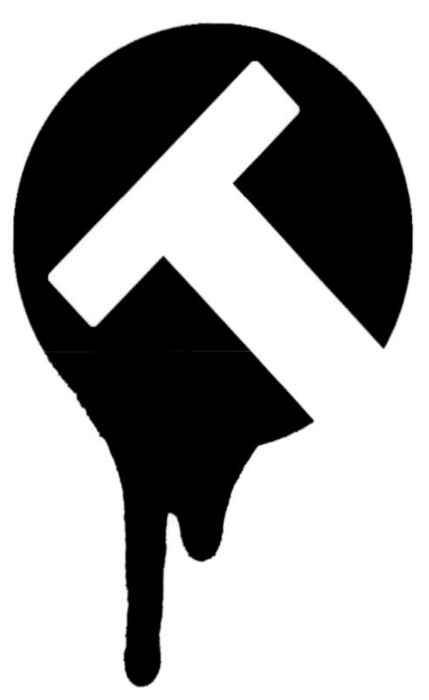

First edition of 500 copies published 2010 by Tangent Books
ISBN: 978-1-906477-38-7

Second edition published 2011 by Tangent Books
ISBN 978-1-906477-53-0

This edition published 2017 by Tangent Books
ISBN 978-1-910089-68-2

Tangent Books
Unit 5.16 Paintworks, Bristol BS4 3EH
0117 972 0645
www.tangentbooks.co.uk
richard@tangentbooks.co.uk

ISBN 978-1-910089-68-2

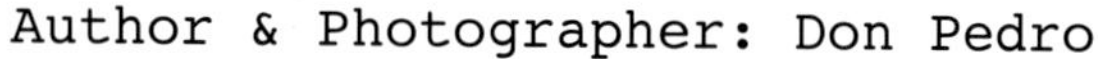

Author & Photographer: Don Pedro

Design: Joe Burt (joe@wildsparkdesign.com)

A CIP record of this book is available at the British Library.

Printed on paper from a sustainable source

CLIMATE
CHAOS
AHEAD